ANCIENT FUTURES

Learning from Ladakh

HELENA NORBERG-HODGE

SIERRA CLUB BOOKS   SAN FRANCISCO

Library of Congress Cataloging-in-Publication Data

Norberg-Hodge, Helena.
    Ancient futures : learning from Ladakh / Helena Norberg-Hodge.
        p.   cm.
    Includes index.
    ISBN 0-87156-643-5
    1. Rural development projects—India—Ladakh.   2. Appropriate technology—India—Ladakh.   3. Ladakh (India)—Rural conditions.
    I. Title.
HN690.L33N67   1991
307.1'412'09546—dc20   91-13868
                                                    CIP

Book production by Susan Ristow
Cover design by Laurie Dolphin
Book design by Wilsted & Taylor
Drawings by Thubstan Paldan
Photographs by Helena Norberg-Hodge and John Page

10   9   8   7   6   5

To John and to Marion,
for their love and support,
and to the people of Ladakh,
from whom I have learned so much.

ACKNOWLEDGMENTS

This book could not possibly have been written without the help of all my Ladakhi friends. They are unfortunately far too many to be mentioned individually. However, I owe a special thanks to Tashi Rabgyas and Gyelong Thubstan Paldan, who have guided me for more than fifteen years, and to Sonam Dawa, for his valuable comments and criticisms; to Tsewang Rigzin Lagrook, for his quiet wisdom and compassion, which embodies for me everything that Ladakh represents; and to Sonam Wangchuk and Sonam Dorje of SECMOL, for the hope they offer for Ladakh's future.

John Page, my partner in all things, has provided patient support and advice from beginning to end, while Hildur Jackson gave me the confidence to believe in the book, and helped to put the first draft on paper.

Ian Worrall devoted many years to making the appropriate technology program in Ladakh a reality, and I will always be appreciative of his dedication and skill.

I am also very grateful to my friend Peter Matthiessen for his help and advice, and to Susan Moon, Jonathan Woodbridge, and Peter Goering, who put so much care and energy into helping to make my ideas come alive.

Dorothy Schwartz, Steve Gorelick, Leslie Boies, and Matthew Akester helped to give the book shape; Brian Cooke, Smittu Kothari, Tessa Strickland, Peter Bunyard, Jane Spiro, Stephan Harding, and Anna McKenzie assisted on individual chapters. I am also indebted to Kirkpatrick Sale, Mark Power, Ernest Callenbach, Henry Osmaston, Jane Lury, Eleanor LeCain, and John Elford, for reviewing the entire manuscript.

For secretarial assistance, I would like to thank Elaine Amaron, who typed and retyped numerous drafts, Lena Hadden, Felicity Wight, and my students at Schumacher College in England—Ginny Keegan, Casuarina Mohrmann, Bridget Williamson, Natasha Arnold, Raya van Ingen, and Anthony Whitworth.

I owe a great deal to Mary Anne Stewart. Her enthusiasm and interest in the book pushed me to get it finished. Finally, I want to thank my friend and editor, Danny Moses.

NOTE: I have changed most of the personal names in the book, in order to protect privacy.

CONTENTS

PREFACE

by H. H. The Dalai Lama

Helena Norberg-Hodge has long been a friend of Ladakh and its people. In this book she expresses her deep appreciation for the traditional Ladakhi way of life, as well as some concern for its future.

Like Tibet and the rest of the Himalayan region, Ladakh lived a self-contained existence, largely undisturbed for centuries. Despite the rigorous climate and the harsh environment, the people are by and large happy and contented. This is no doubt due partly to the frugality that comes of self-reliance and partly to the predominantly Buddhist culture. The author is right to highlight the humane values of Ladakhi society, a deep-rooted respect for each other's fundamental human needs and an acceptance of the natural limitations of the environment. This kind of responsible attitude is something we can all admire and learn from.

The abrupt changes that have taken place in Ladakh in recent decades are a reflection of a global trend. As our world grows smaller, previously isolated peoples are inevitably being brought into the greater human family. Naturally, adjustment takes time, in the course of which there is bound to be change.

I share the author's concern for the threatened ecology of our planet and admire the work she has done in promoting alternative solutions to many of the problems of modern development. If the Ladakhis' enduring treasure, their natural sense of responsibility for each other and their environment, can be maintained and reapplied to new situations, then I think we can be optimistic about Ladakh's future. There are young Ladakhis who have completed a modern education and are prepared to help their own people. At the same time traditional education has been strengthened in the monastic system through the restoration of links with Tibetan monasteries reestablished in exile. Finally, Ladakh has an abundance of sympathetic friends from abroad, who, like the author, are ready to offer support and encouragement.

No matter how attractive a traditional rural society may seem, its people cannot be denied the opportunity to enjoy the benefits of modern development. However, as this book suggests, development and learning should not take place in one direction only. Amongst the people of traditional societies such as Ladakh's there is often an inner development, a sense of warm-heartedness and contentment, that we would all do well to emulate.

February 26, 1991

INTRODUCTION

by Peter Matthiessen

Ladakh, under Karakoram, in the trans-Himalayan region of Kashmir, is a remote region of broad arid valleys set about with peaks that rise to 20,000 feet. It lies in the great rainshadow north of the Himalayan watershed, in a sere land of wind, high desert, and remorseless sun. It is easier to travel north into Tibet than south across the Himalayas to the subcontinent, and the people speak a dialect of the Tibetan tongue. Like Assam, Bhutan, the Mustang and Dolpo regions of northern Nepal, and other mountainous regions of the great Himalayan frontier, Ladakh for the past one thousand years has been an enclave of Tibetan Buddhism.

Politically, *La dags,* the Land, is a semi-autonomous district divided (by the British-administered partition of 1947) between Muslim Pakistan and Hindu India. Culturally, it is far more ancient, a two-thousand-year-old kingdom of Tatar herders who have learned how to grow barley and a few other hardy crops—peas, turnips, potatoes—in the brief growing season at these high altitudes. Black walnut trees and apricots are maintained at the lower elevations. The doughty way of Ladakhi life is made possible by skillful use of the thin soil and scarce water, and by hardy domestic animals—sheep, goats, a few donkeys and small shaggy horses, and in particular the *dzo,* a governable hybrid of archaic Asian cattle with the cantankerous semi-wild black ox known as the yak. These animals furnish a resourceful folk with meat and milk, butter and cheese, draft labor and transport, wool, and fuel. In a treeless land, the dried dung cakes of the cattle, gathered all year, are a precious resource, supplying not only cooking fuel but meager heat in the long winters in which temperatures may fall to −40°F.

Until recent years, essential needs of the Ladakhis—housing, clothes, and food—were produced locally, by hand, and so a precious resource is communal labor, which is given generously for house construction (stones and mud, whitewashed with lime) or in harvest season, or for tending herds. The high altitudes are greener than the valley floor, and the herds, taken to high pastures in the summer, are thereby kept away from the small barley fields and vegetable gardens. Livestock manure is gathered for cooking fuel and winter heating, and human waste, mixed with ash and earth, is spread upon the gardens; there is no pollution. Thus nothing is wasted and nothing thrown away; a use is found for everything.

In the very grain of Ladakhi life are the Buddhist teachings, which decry waste, and encourage the efficient husbanding of land and water—a frugality, as Helena Norberg-Hodge points out, that has nothing to do with stinginess (also decried in Buddhist teachings) but arises, rather, from respect and gratitude for the limited resources of the land. Water is drawn carefully from glacial brooks—one stream may be reserved for drinking, the next for washing. Indeed, it is pains-taking attention to each object and each moment that makes possible this self-sustaining culture that nonetheless provides Ladakhis with much leisure time.

Watching a mother and her two daughters watering, I saw them open small channels and, when the ground was saturated, block them with a spadeful of earth. They managed to spread the water remarkably evenly, knowing just where it would flow easily and where it would need encouragement. A spadeful dug out here, put back there; a rock shifted just enough to open a channel. All this with the most delicate sense of timing. From time to time they would lean on their spades and chat with their neighbors, with one eye on the water's progress.

Like the Hopi and other AmerIndian peoples (now thought to have come from the same regions near Lake Baikal and the Gobi Desert as the Tatar peoples who came later to this Himalayan region), the Ladakhis share the Tibetan perception of a circular reality, with life and death as "two aspects of an ever-returning process," and even in certain details of material culture, comparisons with AmerIndian ways are very interesting. The barley farina known in Ladakh as *ngamphe* is called *tsampa* in Tibetan; a very similar corn farina made in America by Algonkian peoples is called *samp*.

Even if *samp-tsampa* were mere coincidence, other parallels are not easily dismissed, such as the custom that a habitation should face east toward the sunrise, the prohibition against telling tales in winter, certain healing techniques mysterious to Westerners, and the profound respect for old people and children, who are welcomed to each activity of every day. In AmerIndian tribes of the Amazonian basin, one may be banished into the surrounding forest for displaying anger; *schon chan* (one who angers easily) is one of the worst insults in the Ladakhi language. Rather than fume when put upon, as Westerners might do, the Ladakhi says, *Chi choen*—What's the point? "Lack of pride" is a virtue, for pride, born of ego, has nothing to do with self-respect among these Buddhist people; I witnessed this repeatedly in Himalayan travels with Sherpas (in Tibetan, "easterners") and the folk of Dolpo, who like the Ladakhis live a pure Tibetan Buddhist culture.

Though I have never found the opportunity to travel to Ladakh since the author first invited me ten years ago, the aesthetic and spiritual correspondences between this land and Dolpo are very obvious in her account. Both are dry, fierce, all but treeless mountain landscapes set about with *stupas* and *chortens*, prayer flags and cairns, and prayer walls of carved stones. The dominant wild animals are the blue sheep (actually a goat), Asian wolf, and snow leopard. The author describes the experience of a Ladakhi shepherdess tending her sheep along a ravine:

Just above the path, a ball of burtse, *a shrub that is used as fuel, began rolling down the scree: not bouncing, as you would expect, but gliding smoothly, even over bumpy stones. It surprised her; she had never seen anything like this before. Puzzled, she watched it roll closer. As it came to a standstill a few yards from the animals, it looked up at her, this shrub, and she suddenly realized what it was—a snow leopard.*

The celebration here of traditional Ladakhi life induces exhilaration but also sadness, as if some half-remembered paradise known in another life had now been lost. So evocative is it that I felt—I'm not sure what—*homesickness* for the Crystal Monastery? Or perhaps a memory of "homegoing," as if I were returning to lost paradise, that ancient and harmonious way of life that even Westerners once knew—and indeed still know—in the farthest corners of old Europe.

The Ladakhis' attitude to life—and death—seems to be based on an intuitive understanding of impermanence and a consequent lack of attachment. . . . Rather than clinging to an idea of how things should be, they seem blessed with an ability to actively welcome things as they are . . .

It is easy to romanticize self-sufficient economies and traditional technologies, and it is also easy, as the author makes clear, to ignore their benefits, from the consolations of working the soil with draft animals rather than tractors to grinding grain with water-powered wheels instead of engines. Many archaic societies are more sustainable than our own in terms of their relationship with the earth, and their patterns of living more conducive to psychological balance— "more in touch," as the author says, "with our own human nature, showing us that peace and joy can be a way of life." Anyone with experience of such societies can testify that this thinking is neither wishful nor romantic. Anyway, Ms. Norberg-Hodge is essentially pragmatic and hard-headed:

"[The] one-dimensional view of progress, widely favored by economists and development experts, has helped to mask the negative impact of economic growth. . . . This has led to a grave misunderstanding of the situation of the majority of people on earth today—the millions in the rural sector of the Third World—and has disguised the fact that development programs, far from benefiting these people, have, in many cases, served only to lower their standard of living."

Modern technologies, based on capital and fossil fuels, lead inevitably to centralization and specialization, to cash crops as opposed to subsistence agriculture and barter, to time-wasting travel and stressful town life among strangers. And they are labor-saving only in the narrowest sense, since gaining one's livelihood in the new ways, which are competitive rather than communal, demands more time. Dependence on international trade for goods and materials leads inevitably to a monoculture—the same sources and resources for both material and abstract needs, from dress to music—and, increasingly, a common language (a pauperized English, in most cases), and even a common education and set of values, with corresponding dismissal and even contempt for the local culture. Modern education tends to belittle local resources, teaching children to find inferior not only their traditional culture but themselves.

Meanwhile, the intense competition that replaces barter and communal effort leads inevitably to increasing dissatisfaction, greed, dispute, and even war, all on behalf of an economic model that the local people cannot emulate and that, even if they could, would almost certainly be inappropriate for Ladakh (and other Third World lands of narrow resources). Yet the future of such countries lies entirely in the hands of development corporations and financial institutions, including the World Bank, where decisions are based on Western economic systems rather than the welfare of the client states.

Another unfortunate consequence of disruption is population increase, which underlies the breakdown of cultures the world over. Until recent years, the Ladakhi population was well adjusted to the limited amount of arable land and the slender resources of water and stock forage. The increasing dependence on the outside world, the author says, "erodes personal responsibility and clouds the fact that resources are limited. Optimists assume that we will be able to invent our way out of any resource shortage, that science will somehow stretch the earth's bounty ad infinitum. Such a view is a denial of the fact that there are limits in the natural world which are beyond our power to change, and conveniently circumvents the need for a redistribution of wealth. A change in the global economy is not necessary if you believe that there is going to be more and more to go around."

Is it (as suggested here) that the would-be corporate developers and the would-be benefactors, with their inappropriate technologies, are out of touch with reality, or is it that, while quite aware—indeed, more aware than anybody else—of the debt, dependence, and environmental pollution being inflicted on a formerly clean and self-reliant culture, they pursue nonetheless the easy short-term profit, leaving behind not just pollution but frustration, misery, and anger? For the ethical basis of traditional Buddhist belief, based on the unity and mutual interdependence of all life, is grievously missing from the Western codes that now impinge upon the people of Ladakh.

The Buddhist ability to adjust to any situation, to feel happy regardless of circumstances, is already eroded, and so is that "deep-rooted contentedness that they took for granted." Only sixteen years ago, when Helena Norberg-Hodge first went to Ladakh, the people would not sell their old wood butter jars no matter what was offered by their few visitors; today, only too eager to sell, they store their butter in tin cans.

From a social point of view, the losses that accrue to misguided development may become even more painful than the material ones. As the author demonstrates, the small communities and large extended families of Ladakhi life are a better foundation for "growing up" than the unnatural alienation of leaving home, which leads, paradoxically, to clinging and grasping attitudes and relationships that directly contravene the Buddhist teachings. In addition to the contempt for one's own culture, the aspiration for what one is taught to want but will never (in the great majority of cases) have is encouraged by misplaced technological progress and its many ills. With the advent of specialization, work is done away from home, social life depends on business associates and strangers, and the children are increasingly excluded. The culture fragments at an ever-increasing rate, as so-called "progress" divides the Ladakhis from their native earth, from one another, and from what Buddhists call "their own true nature."

As Wendell Berry has written in *The Unsettling of America*:

What happens under the rule of specialization is that, though society becomes more and more intricate, it has less and less structure. It becomes more and more organized, but less and less orderly. The community disintegrates because it loses the necessary understandings, forms and enactments of the relations among materials and processes, principles and actions, ideals and realities, past and present, present and future, men and women, body and spirit, city and country, civilization and wilderness, growth and decay, life and death—just as the individual character loses the sense of a responsible involvement in these relationships . . .

The only possible guarantee of the future is responsible behavior in the present. When supposed future needs are used to justify misbehavior in the present, as is the tendency with us, then we are both perverting the present and diminishing the future . . .

Although responsible use may be defined, advocated, and to some extent required by organizations, it cannot be implemented or enacted by them. It cannot be effectively enforced by them. The use of the world is finally a personal matter, and the world can be preserved in health only by the forbearance and care of a multitude of persons.

Helena Norberg-Hodge is certainly one of those persons, and her valuable book cries out to those who are not. On occasion over the years, I have attended her eloquent public appeals, and know how effective an advocate she is, not only because of her intelligence and sincerity and presence but because of a profound commitment that has taken her to Ladakh for half the year for the past sixteen years.

A highly trained linguist who had studied in five countries and spoke six languages, she learned the Ladakhi dialect in her first year, and since then she has informed herself in all the societal, environmental, and alternative energy disciplines that she had to understand in order to establish the remarkable Ladakh Project, set up "to warn the Ladakhis of the long-term 'side-effects' of conventional development and to present practical alternatives, from the demonstration of solar heating systems to educational programs for schoolchildren." Since its founding, the Project has earned the strong endorsement of numerous world figures. *Ancient Futures* reveals a knowledge of certain complex principles of Buddhist doctrine that permit her to understand this ancient social order that much better—the humanism of old ways *that worked,* emotionally as well as economically, now threatened with fatal loss by ways that don't.

This is not to say that the pervasive human well-being in Ladakh is gone forever. Indeed, it is one of the virtues of this book that it points to real solutions, and ends on an inspiring note of hope and determination. As the author suggests, we have much to learn from Ladakhi culture, and we will ignore these teachings at our peril.

ANCIENT FUTURES

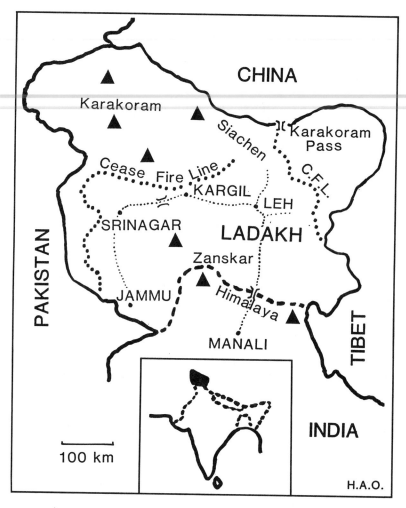

100 km

H.A.O.

Ladakh is a part of the Indian state of Jammu and Kashmir. It is divided into two districts: Leh, which is primarily Buddhist, and Kargil, which is largely Muslim. The whole region covers an area of 40,000 square miles, and supports a population of approximately 130,000.

This book focuses on the region's Buddhist culture, based on the author's experiences in the Leh District and the Zanskar Valley of Kargil. For the sake of convenience, the term "Ladakh" is generally used in the text to refer to these two "sub-regions."

LEARNING FROM LADAKH

Why is the world teetering from one crisis to another? Has it always been like this? Were things worse in the past? Or better?

Experiences over more than sixteen years in Ladakh, an ancient culture on the Tibetan Plateau, have dramatically changed my response to these questions. I have come to see my own industrial culture in a very different light.

Before I went to Ladakh, I used to assume that the direction of "progress" was somehow inevitable, not to be questioned. As a consequence, I passively accepted a new road through the middle of the park, a steel-and-glass bank where the two-hundred year old church had stood, a supermarket instead of the corner shop, and the fact that life seemed to get harder and faster with each day. I do not any more. Ladakh has convinced me that there is more than one path into the future and given me tremendous strength and hope.

In Ladakh I have had the privilege to experience another, saner way of life and to see my own culture from the outside. I have lived in a society based on fundamentally different principles and witnessed the impact of the modern world on that culture. When I arrived as one of the first outsiders in several decades, Ladakh was still essentially unaffected by the West. But change came swiftly. The collision between the two cultures has been particularly dramatic, providing stark and vivid comparisons. I have learned something about the psychology, values, and social and technological structures that support our industrialized society and about those that support an ancient, nature-based society. It has been a rare opportunity to compare our socioeconomic system with another, more fundamental, pattern of existence—a pattern based on a coevolution between human beings and the earth.

Through Ladakh I came to realize that my passivity in the face of destructive change was, at least in part, due to the fact that I had confused culture with nature. I had not realized that many of the negative trends I saw were the result of my own industrial culture, rather than of some natural, evolutionary force beyond our control. Without really thinking about it, I also assumed that human beings were essentially selfish, struggling to compete and survive, and that more cooperative societies were nothing more than utopian dreams.

It was not strange that I thought the way I did. Even though I had lived in many different countries, they had all been industrial cultures. My travels in less "developed" parts of the world, though fairly extensive, had not been enough to afford me an inside view. Some intellectual travels, like reading Aldous Huxley and Erich Fromm, had opened a few doors, but I was essentially a product of industrial society, educated with the sort of blinders that every culture employs in order to perpetuate itself. My values, my understanding of history, my thought patterns all reflected the world view of homo industrialis.

Mainstream Western thinkers from Adam Smith to Freud and today's academics tend to universalize what is in fact Western or industrial experience. Explicitly or implicitly, they assume that the traits they describe are a manifestation of human nature, rather than a product of industrial culture. This tendency to generalize from Western experience becomes almost inevitable as Western culture reaches out from Europe and North America to influence all the earth's people.

Every society tends to place itself at the center of the universe and to view other cultures through its own colored lenses. What distinguishes Western culture is that it has grown so widespread and so powerful that it has lost a perspective on itself; there is no "other" with which to compare itself. It is assumed that everyone either is like us or wants to be.

Most Westerners have come to believe that ignorance, disease, and constant drudgery were the lot of preindustrial societies, and the poverty, disease, and starvation we see in the developing world might at first sight seem to substantiate this assumption. The fact is, however, that many, if not most of the problems in the "Third World" today are to a great extent the consequences of colonialism and misguided development.

Over the last decades, diverse cultures from Alaska to Australia have been overrun by the industrial monoculture. Today's conquistadors are "development," advertising, the media, and tourism. Across the world, "Dallas" beams into people's homes and pinstripe suits are de rigueur. This year I have seen almost identical toy shops appear in Ladakh and in a remote mountain village of Spain. They both sell the same blonde, blue-eyed Barbie dolls and Rambos with machine guns.

The spread of the industrial monoculture is a tragedy of many dimensions. With the destruction of each culture, we are erasing centuries of accumulated knowledge, and as diverse ethnic groups feel their identity threatened, conflict and social breakdown almost inevitably follow.

Increasingly, Western culture is coming to be seen as the normal way, the only way. And as more and more people around the world become competitive, greedy, and egotistical, these traits tend to be attributed to human nature. Despite persistent voices to the contrary, the dominant thinking in Western society has long assumed that we are indeed aggressive by nature, locked in a perpetual Darwinian struggle. The implications of this view for the way we structure our society are of fundamental importance. Our assumptions about human nature, whether we believe in inherent good or evil, underlie our political ideologies and thus help to shape the institutions that govern our lives.

In our mainstream culture we blame innate human failings for our problems, while ignoring our own hand in the structural changes called "development" or "progress." Technological development is seen as part of a continuum of evolutionary change. In the same way as human beings evolved over the millennia—starting to walk upright, to use language, to create artifacts—so, it is thought, they have invented the atom bomb and biotechnology. We do not distinguish between evolution and the changes wrought by the scientific revolution, forgetting that while Europe was transformed by industrialization, the majority of the world continued to live according to other principles and values. In so doing, we are effectively saying that Westerners are more highly evolved than traditional peoples.

We treat technological change as more natural than the changing weather, and seem locked into the belief that wherever scientific inventiveness goes, we must follow. This is not to deny that human nature has a dark side or that the process of development has brought benefits, but Ladakh has shown me that this process exacerbates greed, competition, and aggression while vastly increasing the potential for destruction. It was never previously possible to affect the climate, to poison the seas, or to eradicate forests, animal species, and cultures at the rate that we are doing today. The scale and the speed of our destructive power has never been so great. There is no historical precedent. Our situation is unique, and time is not on our side.

Large-scale environmental destruction, inflation, and unemployment are the consequences of a technoeconomic dynamic that has little to do with "right" or "left" politics. In a fundamental way, the world has experienced only one development model, based on one type of science and technology. The consequent specialization and centralization have led to a dramatic transformation of life that has outweighed and overshadowed the differences between capitalism and communism.

In Ladakh I have known a society in which there is neither waste nor pollution, a society in which crime is virtually nonexistent, communities are healthy and strong, and a teenage boy is never embarrassed to be gentle and affectionate with his mother or grandmother. As that society begins to break down under the pressures of modernization, the lessons are of relevance far beyond Ladakh itself.

It may seem absurd that a "primitive" culture on the Tibetan Plateau could have anything to teach our industrial society. Yet we need a baseline from which to better understand our own complex culture. In Ladakh I have seen progress divide people from the earth, from one another, and ultimately from themselves. I have seen happy people lose their serenity when they started living according to our norms. As a result, I have had to conclude that culture plays a far more fundamental role in shaping the individual than I had previously thought.

At the moment, an increasingly narrow view prevents us from seeing the roots of many of our problems; we cannot see the forest for the trees. Western culture depends on experts whose focus of attention grows more and more specialized and immediate at the expense of a broader, long-term perspective. Economic forces are pulling the world rapidly toward ever-greater specialization and centralization and an ever more capital- and energy-intensive pattern of life.

We urgently need to steer toward a sustainable balance—a balance between urban and rural, male and female, culture and nature. Ladakh can help to show the way, by giving us a deeper understanding of the interrelated forces that are shaping our society. This wider perspective is, I believe, an essential step in learning how to heal ourselves and the planet.

PART ONE

TRADITION

CHAPTER ONE

LITTLE TIBET

If the place is not recognized
It is from where the whole land is seen
The Gesar Saga

The rough, winding road from Srinagar leads to Leh, capital of the old kingdom of Ladakh. It climbs through the moss green pine forests of Kashmir to the Zoji-la pass, a dramatic boundary between two worlds. Ahead of you, in the parched rainshadow of the Himalayas, the earth is bare. In every direction are mountains, a vast plateau of crests in warm and varied tones from rust to pale green. Above, snowy peaks reach toward a still, blue sky; below, sheer walls of wine red scree fall to stark lunar valleys.

How can life be sustained in this wilderness? Everything is barren; each step you take sends up a cloud of sand and dust. Yet as your eyes begin to comprehend what they see, brilliant green oases come into focus, set like emeralds in a vast elephant-skin desert.

Fields of barley appear, fringed with wild flowers and herbs and the clear waters of glacial streams. Above the fields sits a cluster of houses, gleaming white, three floors high, and hung with finely carved balconies; brightly colored prayer flags flutter on the roof-tops. Higher still, perched on the mountainside, a monastery watches over the village.

As you wander through the fields, or follow the narrow paths that wind between the houses, smiling faces greet you. It seems impossi-

ble that people could prosper in such desolation, and yet all the signs
are that they do. Everything has been done with care: fields have been
carved out of the mountainside and layered in immaculate terraces,
one above the other; the crops are thick and strong and form such
patterns that an artist might have sown their seeds.

Around each house, vegetables and fruit trees are protected from
the goats by a stone wall on which cakes of dung, to be used as fuel for
the kitchen stove, lie baking in the sun. On the flat roof, animal fodder—alfalfa and hay, together with leaves of the wild iris—has been
stacked in neat bundles for winter. Apricots left to dry on yak-hair
blankets and potted marigolds give a blaze of brilliant orange.

The name Ladakh is probably derived from the Tibetan *la-dags,*
meaning "land of mountain passes." Lying in the shadow of the Himalayas, Ladakh is a high-altitude desert, criss-crossed by giant mountain ranges. Its first inhabitants are thought to have been two Aryan
groups, the Mons of northern India and the Dards of Gilgit, who
were at a very early stage (possibly about 500 B.C.) joined by a larger
group of Mongolian nomads from Tibet. Present-day Ladakhis are
descended from a blend of these three races.

Culturally, Ladakh is Tibetan and is, in fact, often referred to as
Little Tibet. Language, art, architecture, medicine, and music all reflect this heritage. Tibetan Mahayana Buddhism is the predominant
religion, and the Dalai Lama is the spiritual leader. For centuries,
monks from Ladakh studied in Tibetan monasteries, and there was a
constant interchange of both merchandise and ideas.

Despite this close cultural contact with Tibet, Ladakh was an independent kingdom from about A.D. 950 until 1834, when it was invaded by Hindu Dogras. When the Dogras gained control of
Kashmir, Ladakh and neighboring Baltistan fell under the rule of the
Maharaja of Jammu and Kashmir. Following the Indo-Pakistan war of
1947, the Baltistan region lay on the Pakistan side of the cease-fire
line, and the rest of Ladakh became part of the Indian state of Jammu
and Kashmir. Due to increasing tensions between India and Pakistan,
the Chinese invasion of Tibet in the 1950s, and their occupation of

the Aksai Chin region in 1962, Ladakh has become one of India's most important strategic zones.

Life in Ladakh is dictated by the seasons—more so, perhaps, than in almost any other inhabited place on earth. Scorched by the sun in summer, the entire region freezes solid for eight months in winter, when temperatures drop to as low as minus forty degrees. This is the fiercest of climates: winds whip up tornadoes along the empty corridors of desert; rain is so rare that it is easy to forget its very existence.

The vast majority of Ladakhis are self-supporting farmers, living in small settlements scattered in the high desert. The size of each village depends on the availability of water, which comes from the melted snow and ice of the mountains. Generations ago, channels were built, tapping the meltwater from above and bringing it down to the fields. The water is often channeled for several miles, across steep walls of rock and scree, stretching it as far as it will reach. An elaborate, well-maintained network of smaller channels weaves through each village.

At altitudes of 10,000 feet and above, and with a growing season limited to little more than four months, the decision as to what to plant is to a great extent already made for the Ladakhis. As elsewhere on the Tibetan Plateau, the principal crop is barley; the diet is based on its roasted flour, *ngamphe*. About two-thirds of the fields are planted with barley, the remainder with fast-growing varieties of wheat. Most farmers also have some small fields of peas and a garden of turnips. In the valleys below 11,000 feet there are orchards of apricots and giant walnut trees. In the very highest settlements, where not even barley will grow, people depend largely on animal husbandry.

The average family holding is about five acres; occasionally a household might have as many as ten. Optimum acreage is determined by the size of the family, roughly one acre per working member of the household. Beyond that, land is not of much use. There is no point in possessing land you cannot work. (This is reflected in the fact that Ladakhis measure land according to how long it takes to

The village of Photoksar, in Zanskar.

*The village of Mangyoo. Settlements range in size
from one to more than a hundred houses.*

plough it. The size of a plot is described as "one day," "two days," and so on.)

Animals play a central role in the economy. They provide dung, the main fuel, as well as transport, labor, wool, and milk. The most common domesticated animals are sheep, goats, donkeys, horses, cows, and the famous yak. The *dzo,* a hybrid between the local cow and yak, is the most important and useful draft animal.

Vast stretches of grazing land (*phu*), which lie in the vicinity of the glaciers at elevations of 15,000 to 18,000 feet, serve as pasture. Here, during the short summer, wild plants suddenly proliferate, the edelweiss among them. Unlike the temperate regions of Europe, this arid land is greener at high altitudes. It also supports a variety of wildlife, including blue sheep, the reclusive snow leopard, and wolves. From July to September some of the family spend time here, caring for their animals, gathering dung, and making butter and cheese for the winter.

I spent my first years in Ladakh analyzing the language and collecting folk stories for studies at the School of Oriental and African Studies in London. The written language, which is used in all religious texts, is classical Tibetan. Colloquial Ladakhi, described as a dialect of Tibetan, is different enough to be a separate language. Traditionally it was a spoken language only. For much of the time, I worked with a Buddhist monk, Gyelong Paldan, on a Ladakhi-English dictionary, writing the language in Tibetan script for the first time. One of Ladakh's leading scholars, Tashi Rabgyas, became my guide in trying to untangle the complex grammar, one of the world's most complicated. These two soon became my close friends.

Paldan was in his early thirties, soft spoken and serious looking with a razor-sharp, dry wit. He had spent time as a young monk in Sri Lanka, followed by several years at monasteries in central Tibet. Tashi was fifteen years older, and though not a monk, he was Ladakh's most respected Buddhist philosopher. A man of infectious vitality, his wide face was constantly lighting up with a beaming smile. For Tashi, nothing was dull; he would infuse everything, from a discussion of Einstein's theory of relativity to the conjugation of Ladakhi verbs, with bubbling joy. In addition to being a scholar, he was famous throughout Ladakh for his poetry and songs. Shortly after I started working with him he wrote the following song in Ladakhi for me, which he later translated into English:

In great Europe where you were born,
Many free states are flourishing
With immense material prosperity,
Industries and technologies.

More is the worldly pleasure there,
More is the busy life.
More science and literature,
More change in state of affairs.

Though we lack in progress here,
We have happy peace of mind.
Though we have no technologies,
We have way of deeper Dharma.

Our language in Ladakh and Tibet
Is a tongue of wise lamas,
Is a treasure full of Dharma.
No other tongue can be its equal.

To all splendor of phenomena,
Have a look with careful mind.
Is there any sublime meaning?
Not any meaning I have found.

One may possess plenty to consume;
Prosperous pleasure may abound;
One may have great fame and power;
Death is sure to rob him too.

At time of death, except the deeds,
No chance to take a fragment wealth.
The good and bad acts that we do
Create our joy or sorrow.

If Dharmic essence is not realized,
Dual delusion will remain.
Until understanding transcends speech,
No end to words of terminology.

Now work hard with concentration.
You will learn it before long.
You will see the spectacle.
My claim will also become clear.

While the Ladakhi language remained the primary focus of my work, I was becoming increasingly fascinated by the people, by their values and the way they saw the world. Why were they always smiling? And how did they support themselves in relative comfort in such a hostile environment?

My first real introduction to traditional life came from Sonam, a young man from the village of Hemis Shukpachan. At about five feet two, he was quite short and everyone called him *Baloo,* meaning dwarf. Sonam worked as a clerk at the Department of Education in Leh, while his family all lived back in the village. Not long after my arrival, he was going back home and invited me to join him.

We went first to the monastery of Ridzong, to meet Sonam's brother Thundup, who was the *gonyer,* or key keeper, there. Of all the monasteries in Ladakh, Ridzong is the most respected. The monks belong to the Yellow Hat sect of Tibetan Mahayana Buddhism, established by the great reformer Tsongkapa in the sixteenth century and generally regarded as stricter and more disciplined than the older Red Hat sects. Ridzong is known to be stricter than most.

The monastery is an awe-inspiring building, set so deeply into the barren mountains that stretch in endless silence beyond it that its massive white walls, splashed with deep maroon, could be part of the rock itself. The steep zigzag path that took us from the valley floor up the mountainside to the entrance of the monastery was lined with red-robed figures. It looked like a procession at first, but when we came nearer we saw monks heaving stones and shoveling away mounds of mud and scree; a storm had washed away part of the path. Having heard so much about the exceptional asceticism of these monks, I was amazed to see them joking with one another and singing as they worked.

From Ridzong it was a four-hour walk to Hemis Shukpachan. One of the monks came with us—an old man, also from Hemis, named Norbu. He had a balding head and a contagious smile that revealed sparkling teeth. Our route crossed a pass at a height of 13,000 feet; the land was barren, the rock and sand heated by the sun. Norbu had a headache, yet, still smiling, he had the energy to stitch some colored prayer flags printed with mantras and the sacred Wind Horse (*Lhungsta*) onto the cairn at the top of the pass. Below us lay the village fields, coiled like a green iridescent snake between mountains of purple scree.

The path was steep and rocky, yet the Ladakhis ambled down it as if it were paved. The village of Hemis came up toward us: poplar trees, tall and straight; whitewashed houses golden bright in the evening sun, set in a patchwork of a hundred different greens of ripening crops. We wound between drystone walls that had been built over generations to retain the fragile soil of the mountains. Entering the village itself, in keeping with religious custom, we had to make a slight detour to pass to the left of a *chorten,* the ever-present symbol of Tibetan Buddhism.

*Chorten*s, like giant pawns from a chessboard, grace the entrance to every village, growing out of the soil as inevitably as the mountains themselves. Usually made of whitewashed stone and mud, they taper upward twenty feet or so to a spire. The whole structure represents the fundamentals of Buddhist teachings. A crescent moon cradling the sun at the very top symbolizes the oneness of life, the cessation of duality, thus reminding passers-by that all things, even the sun and the moon, which seem so far apart, are inextricably related.

When we reached the village, we walked up narrow paths between large, flat-roofed houses, passing vegetable gardens and apricot orchards. Children came running up, friendly and unfrightened. Women were spinning wool, talking cheerfully, some with bright-cheeked babies at their breasts. I saw old men with faces of a

Chortens, or stupas, ubiquitous symbols of Tibetan Buddhism.

thousand wrinkles, young girls with long dark hair in thick plaits, a newborn calf nuzzling a goat. *"Jule, karu skyodat-le?"* was the universal greeting. "Hello, how are you?" (or literally, "Where are you going?").

Arriving at Sonam's house, we climbed a flight of stone steps to the first floor. He then took me into the kitchen, a room that was so dark compared with the light outside that for a moment I saw little. In this large room, at least thirty feet across, the windows were small openings in the thick walls and the air was smoky from the fire of the cooking stove. Rows of gleaming brass and copper pots shone brilliantly against dark walls.

Sonam's mother, Tsering Dolkar, stirred a huge pot on the stove. With a nod of the head and a warm smile she welcomed us while Sonam explained who I was. He insisted that I sit next to the stove, the place of honor usually reserved for Grandfather. We sat on padded carpets, arranged in an L-shape along the walls, with low tables, or *chogtse,* in front of us, and drank the renowned salty butter tea—an acquired taste! The teapot was made of brass engraved with graceful patterns and inlaid with silver, its handle and spout shaped in the form of a dragon. Sonam's uncle Phuntsog was rocking a little girl to sleep. He padded back and forth, carrying the girl in a cloth on his back. Abi-le, or Grandmother, was chanting a mantra, her hands gliding across well-worn wooden prayer beads in her lap. *"Om mani padme hum, Om mani padme hum . . ."* I felt at ease with these people, at the quiet and matter-of-fact way in which they accepted the presence of a stranger—as if I had sat in that kitchen many times before.

CHAPTER TWO

LIVING WITH THE LAND

May the crop grow so heavy that it lies down in the furrow!
May it grow so thick that even a hundred young men cannot cut it!
So heavy that a hundred young maidens cannot carry it away!
Ladakhi sowing song

In Ladakh, the agricultural cycle begins sometime between February and June, depending on the altitude. Sowing is a time of lyrical beauty. The sun's arc is higher now, and the valley alive once more. On an eastern exposure high above the village, a large pile of stones in the form of an obelisk (*nyitho*) acts as an agricultural calendar. The point on which its shadow falls below determines when various activities should start. Sowing, irrigating, harvesting may all be represented by specific landmarks. When the sun reaches the right place for sowing, the astrologer is consulted. He studies his charts to ensure that work begins on an auspicious day; hopefully he will be able to match the elements of Earth and Water. Someone whose signs he deems favorable is chosen to sow the first seed.

Next, the spirits of the earth and water—the *sadak* and the *lhu*—must be pacified: the worms of the soil, the fish of the streams, the soul of the land. They can easily be angered; the turning of a spade, the breaking of stones, even walking on the ground above them can upset their peace. Before sowing, a feast is prepared in their honor. For an entire day a group of monks recites prayers; no one eats meat or drinks *chang* (the local barley beer). In a cluster of trees at the edge

19

of the village, where a small mound of clay bricks has been built for the spirits, milk is offered. As the sun sets, other offerings are thrown into the stream.

Some weeks earlier, manure has been brought on the backs of donkeys and placed in heaps beside the fields. Now, at dawn, the women quickly spread it in the furrow. As the sun appears, the whole family gathers. Two men carry the wooden plough; ahead a pair of massive *dzo* dwarf the children who lead them. Work and festivity are one. People drink *chang* from silver-lined cups, and the air hums with the sounds of celebration. A monk in robes of deep maroon chants a sacred text; laughter and song drift back and forth from field to field. The ravages of winter are over.

The *dzo* are yoked. They are docile beasts, but proud; they will not be hurried. Casually almost, they pull the plough. Behind, the sower throws the seeds and sings:

> *Manjushri, the embodiment of wisdom, Hark!*
> *The Gods, the* Lhu, *and owner spirits of the Mother Earth, Hark!*
> *May a hundred plants grow from one seed!*
> *May a thousand grow from two seeds!*
> *May all the grains be twins!*
> *Please give enough that we may worship the Buddhas and*
>   *Bodhisattvas,*
> *That we can support the Sangha and give to the poor!*

Once the sowing has been completed, the crop does not need much care—only watering, which is usually done on a rotational basis, sometimes established by dice. In most villages, irrigation is regulated by a *churpon,* who is appointed or elected from within the village. He operates the flow of water, blocking and opening the canals as required. Householders are allotted a certain period of time every week when they can divert the main channels into their own fields.

Watching a mother and her two daughters watering, I saw them open small channels and, when the ground was saturated, block them with a spadeful of earth. They managed to spread the water remarkably evenly, knowing just where it would flow easily and where it would need encouragement: a spadeful dug out here, put back there; a rock shifted just enough to open a channel—all this with the most delicate sense of timing. From time to time they would lean on their spades and chat with their neighbors, keeping one eye on the water's progress.

Harvest is another festive occasion. A line of reapers, old and young, men and women, sing as they cut the crop low to the ground with sickles. In the evening, people gather to sing, drink, and dance. A butter lamp is lit in the kitchen, and garlands of wheat, barley, and peas are wrapped around the wooden pillars.

The crop is piled in sheaves and is then carried off in back-loads to be threshed. A large circle of packed earth about thirty feet in diameter forms the threshing floor. A number of animals, attached in a line to a central pole, trample the crop, bending down to feast on the grain as they walk. *Dzo* are best for this purpose; not only are they vast and heavy, but once stirred, they can happily trudge around and around for hours. Often there will be a combination of animals, as many as twelve or so; the *dzo* will be on the inside, with only a short distance to cover, while horses and donkeys run along on the outside, scampering to keep up. Behind them, the thresher—sometimes a child—shouts words of encouragement and exhorts them in song: "*Ha-lo baldur, ha-lo baldur . . .*" To prevent animal dung from soiling the grain, the thresher carries a wicker basket, catching the dung with dextrous ease before it lands on the ground. A reserve *dzo* stands nearby waiting its turn, while the other animals that have been brought down from the summer pastures munch on the stubble of the fields.

Winnowing is extraordinarily graceful. In perfect, easy rhythm, the crop is scooped up into the air; the chaff blows away on the wind, and the grain falls to the ground. Two people work together, facing each other with wooden forks; they whistle as they work, inviting the wind, and sometimes they sing:

> *Oh, pure goddess of The Winds!*
> *Oh, beautiful goddess of The Winds!*

Carry away the chaff!
Ongsla skyot!
Separate the chaff from the grain!
Where there is no human help
May the gods help us!
Oh, beautiful goddess,
Ongsla skyot!

The grain is then sifted. Before being put into sacks, a little religious figure, or sometimes a painting of one, is ceremoniously placed on top of one pile to bless the harvest.

Sonam had invited me home for Skangsol, the harvest festival. I woke to the fragrant smell of burning *shukpa,* or juniper. Uncle Phuntsog was walking from room to room carrying an incense burner, the scent wafting into every corner. This daily ceremony ensures a spiritual cleansing and is performed in all Buddhist houses.

I walked out onto the balcony. Whole families—grandfathers, parents, children—were working in the fields, some cutting, some stacking, others winnowing. Each activity had its own particular song. The harvest lay in golden stacks, hundreds to a field, hardly allowing the bare earth to show through. A clear light bathed the valley with an intense brilliance. No ugly geometry had been imposed on this land, no repetitive lines. Everything was easy to the eye, calming to the soul.

Farther down the valley, a man sang to his animals as they ploughed his fields:

Oh, you two great bulls, sons of the wild yak!
Your mother may be a cow, but you are like the tiger and the lion!
You are like the eagle, the king of birds!
Aren't you the dancers of the high peaks?
Aren't you the ones who take the mountains on your lap?
Aren't you the ones who drink the ocean in one gulp?
Oh, you two great bulls, Pull! Pull!

Plowing a field of potatoes in early autumn. The dzo, *cross of yak and cow, is the Ladakhis' most valued draft animal.*

Above me on the roof, the deep, rumbling sound of the *zangstung,* eight-foot-long copper horns, signaled that the ceremony was about to begin. Like all religious occasions, this was a social event too, and several guests had already arrived. Men and women were being entertained in separate rooms. They were sitting at low tables intricately carved with dragons and lotus flowers; on the walls were frescoes many generations old. The men wore long homespun robes (*gonchas*), some a natural beige color, some dyed the deep maroon of the hills. Many wore a large turquoise earring and the traditional hairstyle—a plait at the back, with the front of the head shaved. The women were dressed in fuller robes, topped with a waistcoat of brocade. They wore magnificent jewelry—bracelets, rings, necklaces— and dazzling *peraks*, headdresses studded with dozens of turquoises and corals. An older man waved me over to sit down next to him. "This is my new daughter-in-law," he said, introducing me to the others. His eyes sparkled mischievously as they all laughed.

Sonam circled his guests repeatedly, serving tea and *chang*. As he came to fill your glass, you were expected to refuse again and again,

even withdrawing your glass a few inches to prevent him from pouring anything into it, and only then give way. Such polite refusal (*dzangs
choches*) sometimes takes the form of a song between the host and his
guest:

> *I shall not drink more* chang.
> *Only if someone can take the blue skies on his lap will I take* chang.
>
> *The Sun and Moon take the blue skies on their lap.*
> *Drink cool* chang! *Drink! Drink!*
>
> *I shall not drink more* chang.
> *Only if someone can braid the water of the streams will I take*
> chang.
>
> *The fish with golden eyes braid the water of the streams.*
> *Drink cool* chang! *Drink! Drink!*

The monks were performing the ceremony in the family's altar
room, or *tchotkhang*. They had made pyramids of barley dough decorated with butter and flower petals *(storma)* as offerings to the five
Dharmapalas, the protective deities of Buddhism. For two days now,
Sonam's family would celebrate *skangsol;* the harvest was completed,
and the farmer's year was starting a new cycle. Prayers were offered
for the happiness and prosperity not only of this one family, but for
every sentient being in the universe. The muted sounds of the monks'
chanting and the rhythmic beat of the drums could be heard
throughout the village until dark.

Soon after I had arrived in Ladakh, I was washing some clothes in a
stream. Just as I was plunging a dirty dress into the water, a little girl,
no more than seven years old, came by from a village upstream. "You
can't put your clothes in that water," she said shyly. "People down
there have to drink it." She pointed to a village at least a mile farther
downstream. "You can use that one over there; that's just for
irrigation."

I was beginning to learn how Ladakhis manage to survive in such a difficult environment. I was also beginning to learn the meaning of the word *frugality*. In the West, *frugality* conjures up images of old aunts and padlocked pantries. But the frugality you find in Ladakh, which is fundamental to the people's prosperity, is something quite different. Using limited resources in a careful way has nothing to do with miserliness; this is frugality in its original meaning of "fruitfulness": getting more out of little.

Where we would consider something completely worn out, exhausted of all possible worth, and would throw it away, Ladakhis will find some further use for it. Nothing whatever is just discarded. What cannot be eaten can be fed to the animals; what cannot be used as fuel can fertilize the land.

Sonam's grandmother, Abi-le, did not throw away the barley after making *chang* from it. She had already poured water over the boiled and fermented grain to make four separate brews. Then, instead of discarding it, she spread the grain on a yak-hair blanket to dry so it could later be ground for eating. She molded the crushed remains of apricot kernels, a dark brown paste from which oil had already been carefully squeezed, into the form of a small cup; later, when it had hardened, she would use the cup to turn her spindles. She even saved the dishwater, with its tiny bits of food, to provide a little extra nourishment for the animals.

Ladakhis patch their homespun robes until they can be patched no more. When winter demands that they wear two or three on top of each other, they put the best one on the inside to keep it in good condition for special occasions. When no amount of stitching can sustain a worn-out robe, it is packed with mud into a weak part of an irrigation channel to help prevent leakage.

Virtually all the plants, shrubs, and bushes that grow wild, either around the edges of irrigated land or in the mountains—what we would call "weeds"—are gathered and serve some useful purpose. *Burtse* is used for fuel and animal fodder; *yagdzas,* for the roofs of houses; the thorny *tsermang,* for building fences to keep animals out of fields and gardens; *demok,* as a red dye. Others are used for medicine, food, incense, and basket weaving.

The soil in the stables is dug up to be used as fertilizer, thus recycling animal urine. Dung is collected not only from the stables and pens, but also from the pastures. Even human night soil is not wasted. Each house has composting latrines consisting of a small room with a hole in the floor built above a vertical chute, usually one floor high. Earth and ash from the kitchen stove are added, thus aiding chemical decomposition, producing better fertilizer, and eliminating smells. Once a year the latrine is emptied at ground level and the contents used on the fields.

In such ways Ladakhis traditionally have recycled everything. There is literally no waste. With only scarce resources at their disposal, farmers have managed to attain almost complete self-reliance, dependent on the outside world only for salt, tea, and a few metals for cooking utensils and tools.

With each day and new experience in Ladakh, I gained a deeper understanding of what this self-reliance meant. Concepts like "sustainability" and "ecology" had meant little to me when I first arrived. With the years, I not only came to respect the Ladakhis' successful adaptation to nature, but was also forced to reassess the Western lifestyle I had been accustomed to.

Some of my best memories of living closer to nature come from experiences at the high pastures, or *phu*. For the animals too, the *phu* is the promised land. Earlier in the spring, the farmer has sung to them of the pleasures to come:

> *Oh, you beautiful beast, you strong beast!*
> *Your tail is long, and your horns reach to the sky!*
> *Please plough our fields,*
> *Please work hard for us now,*
> *And we will take you to the pastures*
> *Where you can eat long grass and flowers*
> *And do nothing all day!*
> *Oh, you beautiful beast!*

To reach the *phu* at Nyimaling, the "meadow of sun," we had to cross the high Gongmaru La, a 17,500-foot pass. It would be a long day's journey. My friend Tsering and I would be coming back soon, but her sister, Deskit, and the children would stay up there with her uncle Norbu, making butter and cheese and collecting brushwood and dung. Over the summer, they would collect at least a ton of dried dung, to be used for cooking and basic heating in the coldest months of winter. The rest of the family would travel up and back every now and then to bring up bread, flour, and *chang* and to take back to the village what had been gathered.

The morning of our departure we were up early. We loaded the donkeys with things we would need: warm clothes and blankets, sacks of barley flour, salt, tea, and dried apricots. By lunchtime we were nearing the head of the valley and stopped by the side of a melt-water stream. The mountain walls that rose steeply on both sides had shielded us from the harsh sun all morning, so we had made good time. But now it was getting hotter, and everyone welcomed the rest. Some twigs and dung were collected from the side of the path, and Tsering made a small fire. The salty butter tea was particularly welcome; by now I had come to appreciate it. After a long walk in the dry heat, you feel the need to replenish the salt in your body, while your parched lips cry out for the butter to moisten them.

During the afternoon, as we climbed steadily upward, the extraordinary beauty of the silent landscape filled me with a sense of exhilaration and profound joy. Nonetheless exertion at high altitude was difficult and, straining for breath and feeling light-headed, I had to stop for rests. Tsering, Deskit, and the children stopped too, though they all could have easily run up the slope. At sunset, we reached the top of the pass. We stood spellbound, gazing out on a vista of endless peaks and ranges burnished by the last rays of evening sun. We gave the customary cry, *"Kiki soso, lhar gyalo"* ("May the gods be victorious"), and took a few moments' rest at the *lhato,* the cairn with prayer flags that is the beacon of every mountain pass in Ladakh.

We arrived at the first houses of the *phu* in semidarkness; the sun had set, but a glow remained for more than an hour, silhouetting the peaks in Zanskar a hundred miles away. With the darkening sky, stars began to appear. Standing in a doorway, Uncle Norbu surveyed the valley, checking that he had rounded up all the goats; they should be shut away in their pens before nightfall.

Animals play a central role in the Ladakhi economy,
providing meat, dairy products, wool, labor, and fuel.

Sheep, goats, cows, yaks, and *dzo* all spend their summer at Nyi-maling. The sheep and goats are taken to the hillsides above the valley, every day to a different area so as to avoid overgrazing. Meanwhile, the cows wander along the floor of the valley. The *dzo* and yak, always independent, forage up high near the glaciers. Despite their bulk, these majestic animals climb steep mountain walls with great ease and move with surprising speed. In the summer, a lot of time is devoted to tracking the *dzo* down, as they have a habit of wandering off many miles away, sometimes two or three days' walk over high mountain passes. Often they will turn up unexpectedly at the village, having found their way down from the pasturelands. To protect the crops, they are immediately escorted back to the *phu*. From a distance, my eye saw them as nothing more than black dots against the purple scree. But Deskit's ten-year-old son, Angchuk, could not only tell they were *dzo*, as opposed to yaks or cows, but could distinguish his own animals from the others.

Nyimaling: a 21,000-foot peak towering above the bowl of the valley; patches of green, carpets of wild flowers; marmots whistling to each other; the air ringing with the sounds of flutes and young shepherds' songs. For those few days at the *phu,* I glimpsed what life must have been like for thousands of years. The closeness between the people and the land and the animals they depended on was deeply touching—something that had never been part of my life, yet something that felt familiar.

We lived in one of the stone huts that serve as summer dwellings, modest in comparison with the houses of the village. Beyond the low entrance, a small, dark kitchen led on to a storage area, where we kept the sacks of flour we had brought. Dry stone walls and five-foot-high ceilings created a cavelike atmosphere. Yet in the evenings the cramped and smoky room, with a wick-lamp giving off only just enough light to distinguish faces, was filled with a warmth and vitality. We sang, the little ones danced, and there were always stories.

Suddenly there was a crash outside, and we heard Uncle Norbu shouting *"Shangku! Shangku!"* We all ran outside, and at the other side of the pen I saw a dark shadow disappear into the night. A wolf! Norbu got the lamp from inside and took it over to a young calf. All the other animals were at the other side of the pen. The calf would not live long; a huge slice had been carved from its rump as if by a razor. I found myself shaking with horror, yet wondering how teeth could make such a clean cut.

The Ladakhis were calm. Norbu led the calf away to a pen where it could live out its last hours in peace. Back in the kitchen, he explained how he had suddenly seen the wolf just outside the stone walls of the pen where he was leading the goats. He had thrown a stone and missed, and the wolf had stayed there, ripping at the calf. Only when he leapt over the wall and started beating the wolf with a stick did it give up its prey and head off up into the mountains.

Wolves are a constant threat at the *phu,* more for sheep and goats than for the larger animals. Even during the day, when flocks of two or three hundred animals are taken up into the higher reaches of the valley for grazing, the young shepherds have to keep careful watch. I could see Angchuk checking his sling as we talked. I knew that attacks like this had to be accepted in the mountains, but even so the Ladakhis' attitude was remarkable. I saw no sign of bitterness or self-pity. Nothing, it seemed, could affect their equanimity.

Later, Tsering recounted the time she had taken some sheep along a ravine near the *phu*. Just above the path, a ball of *burtse*, a shrub that is used as fuel, began rolling down the scree—not bouncing as you would expect, but gliding smoothly, even over bumpy stones. It surprised her; she had never seen anything like this before. Puzzled, she watched it roll closer. As it came to a standstill a few yards from the animals, it looked up at her, this shrub, and she suddenly realized what it was—a snow leopard. This mythical animal is famous for its ability to disguise itself, and so shy that it is hardly ever seen. But its raids are real enough: some neighbors had lost three sheep only a few weeks before as a leopard managed to squeeze through a small opening into their pen. Only its tracks gave it away.

"Have you tasted all our different dishes—*skyu, chu tagi . . .?*" people would often ask me with a big smile. The question was put as though there were a vast array to choose from. Actually, I thought the choice rather limited—half a dozen different ways of preparing barley and as many different recipes with wheat.

Ladakhis love their food, and though simple, the diet is nourishing. Grain and butter tea form the staple ingredients. Most of the barley is roasted and then ground into flour, making a handy instant food, *ngamphe:* mixed with a liquid—tea, *chang*, or water—it can be eaten right away. The unroasted barley flour is stirred into soup or mixed with the flour of dried peas to make a sort of bread pudding. A thin pancake-shaped bread *(tagi shamo)* cooked on top of the stove and thicker, rounder loaves *(khambit)* that are baked over the ashes are made of wheat flour. Most excess barley—sometimes as much as a quarter of the harvest—becomes *chang*. Even small babies are given a weak brew. The combination of yeast and barley provides an important source of vitamin B in the diet.

Butter tea *(soldja)* is brewed from a type of green tea. The leaves are boiled for about an hour with salt and soda; then butter is added, and the mixture is poured into a long cylindrical wooden churn with the onomatopoeic name *gurgur*. Everyone loves this tea, and all day, even when people are out in the fields, there is a pot at their side, kept warm over a charcoal brazier.

Most milk, *oma*, is made into butter, *mar*. None of the Ladakhi an-

imals produces very much milk, but it is very rich. Yak milk is exceptionally rich, and its butter is a deep creamy yellow. The remaining
buttermilk makes a low-fat cheese, *churpe,* that is dried and hardened
in the sun. *Churpe,* along with a few vegetables, apricots (the only
sweet treat), and dried meat, can be stored for more than a year without spoiling. Some vegetables, like turnips and potatoes, are kept un-
derground in large earth cellars dug beside the house.

Especially in winter, Ladakhis eat meat (goat in particular, but also
yak and *dzo*) presumably because it would be difficult to survive without. Fish is never eaten, as it is thought that if you are going to take a
life, it is better for it to be the life of a large animal that can supply
food for many people; if you ate fish, you would have to take many
more lives. The killing of animals is not taken lightly and is never done
without asking for forgiveness and with much prayer:

> *Those animals which I use for riding and loading,*
> *Which have been killed for me,*
> *All those whose meat I have taken,*
> *May they attain the state of Buddhahood very soon.*

In Hemis, Uncle Phuntsog could often be seen weaving in the shadow
of a big walnut tree outside the house. Surrounded by a large group of
young helpers working the pedals of the loom and listening to his
every word, he told stories interspersed with song. The young ones
constantly plied him with tea and *chang* from the house, and despite
many distractions, he worked remarkably fast—without ever ap-
pearing to—completing a full length of cloth *(snambu)* in a day. (This
is a standard length, about one foot wide and thirty-five *tru* long—*tru*
being the distance between your fingertips and elbow.)

The Ladakhis get wool either from their own animals or by trading
excess grain, at the rate of ten pounds of barley to one pound of
wool. They wash it, spin it, weave it, dye it, and sew it themselves.
Spinning is a constant activity. You see men and women alike spinning
as they walk with loads on their backs; it appears to be a means of re-
laxation, almost a form of meditation. Men spin the coarser hair and
wool of goat and yak, which is used for blankets, shoes, sacks, and
rope; they also do most of the sewing and weaving. Women spin the

finer sheep's-wool for clothing. Some villages have a weaver in almost every household; others have only a few, in which case the weaver works on an exchange basis, getting butter, grain, *chang,* or even wool in return.

I have spent many hours talking and laughing with Ladakhis as their hands busied themselves with this type of work: sitting by the stove in the evening, drinking *chang* together in the fields, or trekking in the mountains. Wool is used to make the men's handsome robes, long and straight, and the women's, gathered into a flowing skirt. Everyone wears tall, sheepskin-lined hats and rather unusual-looking shoes of tie-dyed yak hair that point up at the front.

Jewelry is imported. Every turquoise, every coral represents a surplus of some kind that has been available for trading. Within a single family you may find hundreds of precious stones, as well as silver and gold pendants and conch-shell bracelets.

Village houses are large structures two or three floors high, with a floor area of four thousand square feet or more. Whitened walls slope gently inward toward a flat roof, giving the house grace despite its massive, fortresslike proportions. A new house is never built without concern for the *sadak,* the spirits of the earth. First of all, a high lama comes to bless the land. He then uses a brass mirror to reflect all the surroundings, thus capturing the *sadak* in order to protect them from harm during construction. The mirror is carefully placed in a box, where it remains until the house is finished. At that time there is a final ceremony in which the lama opens the box and sets the spirits free.

Although stone is often used for the first floor, the main building material is mud. Together the whole family prepares the bricks; even small children join in putting mud into the wooden molds. As soil varies from village to village, practices differ: sometimes larger bricks are made, sometimes straw is added to the mix. The bricks are left to dry in the sun and are ready for use after a couple of weeks. Walls are often three feet thick, plastered with a fine clay called *markala* (literally, "butter-mud") and then whitewashed with limestone. Poplar beams, with willow branches placed in a herring-bone pattern across them, form the flat roof. *Yagdzas,* a shrub rather like

A typical house in Hemis Shukpachan. The finely carved
*balconies (*rapsal*) are made by the village carpenter.*

heather, which is said to last for a hundred years, lies on top of the
wood and is packed with mud and earth. Since there is so little pre-
cipitation, any snow is simply brushed off, and it rarely rains enough
to cause leakage.

The house is more than just functional; time is spent on details
that are purely aesthetic. Windows and doors receive special attention. Some have ornately carved lintels (the work of the village carpenter); the most popular design is the lotus. A jet black border,
about ten inches wide and made from a mixture of soot and clay, contrasts with the white walls. Small balconies, again finely worked,
adorn the upper floors.

The entrance to the house faces east, as this is considered auspicious. A stone stairway takes you straight up to the first floor, the
ground floor serving as stables for the animals. Beyond the entrance-
way stretches the kitchen, which, together with the attached storage
rooms, takes up most of the first story; above you, light beams in
from a large courtyard on the second floor.

The kitchen is the heart of the house; here the family spends most
of its time. Kitchens are usually so large that it can be difficult to talk

to someone on the other side of the room. Other than a few low tables and mats, there is little furniture; two-thirds of the floor area is left completely uncluttered. Along one wall, a row of ornate wooden shelves is filled with a dazzling array of pots of every size. A large, shiny black stove is the focal point of every kitchen. Although it looks like wrought iron, it is in fact made of clay. Its sides are decorated with good-luck symbols and other Buddhist motifs, often studded with turquoise and coral. The fire is fed with dried dung and kept alight with goatskin bellows.

Much of the house is given over to storage, as for more than six months of the year nothing grows outside. Off the kitchen is the main storeroom, its thick walls ensuring that it stays icy cool in the heat of summer. It is filled with large wooden barrels for *chang,* clay pots for milk and yoghurt, and vast bins filled with barley and wheat flour. The roof is stacked with alfalfa grass for the animals and shrubs and dung for the kitchen stove. In the summer, yak-hair blankets are always spread out on the roof, with vegetables, apricots, and sometimes cheese drying in the sun.

On the top floor, surrounding the courtyard, are usually two or three rooms—typically the guest room, a summer bedroom, and the family "chapel," the most elaborate and expensive part of the house. The guest room, which is where more formal entertaining goes on, is lavishly decorated and carpeted throughout with Tibetan rugs. The "chapel" is filled with religious texts and other treasures that have been passed on for generations. The strong smell of apricot oil pervades this dark and silent room. Worn *thankas* (religious paintings on cloth) cover the walls, and a large drum hangs from the ceiling. An intricately carved and painted altar is lined with silver bowls and butter lamps. On special days of the Buddhist calendar, monks gather here to perform religious ceremonies, and each morning and evening one of the family makes offerings, lighting the oil-filled lamps, filling the bowls with water, and chanting mantras and prayers.

Despite an extreme climate and a scarcity of resources, Ladakhis enjoy more than mere subsistence—an achievement all the more remarkable since people have only the most basic tools to work with. The only artifact besides the plough and the loom that we might label "technology" is the water mill, an ingeniously simple design complete with a friction-operated grain-release mechanism that obviates the need for supervision. Otherwise, only such implements as spades, saws, sickles, and hammers are used. Nothing more sophisticated is necessary. For many tasks in which we would employ large machinery, Ladakhis have animals and teamwork instead, each task accompanied by song:

Lhamo khyong, Lhamo khyong   ("make it easy, easy does it")
Yale khyong, Lhamo-le

Whole caravans of yak, *dzo,* horses, and donkeys carry most provisions. Bricks and stones are often transported by long lines of people who pass them along one by one; for something like a large tree trunk, groups of men will form a team.

With only simple tools at their disposal, Ladakhis spend a long time accomplishing each task. Producing wool for clothes involves the time-consuming work of looking after the sheep while they graze, shearing them with hand tools, and working the wool from beginning to end—cleaning, spinning, and finally weaving it. In the same way, producing food, from sowing the seed until the food is served on the table, is labor-intensive. Yet I found that the Ladakhis had an abundance of time. They worked at a gentle pace and had a surprising amount of leisure.

Time is measured loosely; there is never a need to count minutes. "I'll come to see you toward midday, toward evening," they will say, giving themselves several hours' leeway. Ladakhi has many lovely words to depict time, all broad and generous. *Gongrot* means "from after dark till bedtime"; *nyitse* means literally "sun on the mountain peaks"; and *chipe-chirrit,* "bird song," describes that time of the morning, before the sun has risen, when the birds sing.

Even during the harvest season, when the work lasts long hours, it is done at a relaxed pace that allows an eighty-year-old as well as a young child to join in and help. People work hard, but at their own rate, accompanied by laughter and song. The distinction between work and play is not rigidly defined.

Remarkably, Ladakhis only work, really work, for four months of the year. In the eight winter months, they must cook, feed the animals, and carry water, but work is minimal. Most of the winter is spent at festivals and parties. Even during summer, hardly a week passes without a major festival or celebration of one sort or another, while in winter the celebration is almost nonstop.

Winter is also the time for telling stories. In fact, there is a saying in Ladakh: "As long as the earth is green, no tale should be told." This prohibition on storytelling in the summer must arise from the need to concentrate on agriculture in those few short months. In the ancient *Gesar* saga, a mythical hero travels far and wide, over many high mountain passes, overcoming demons and saving lives with the help of the gods. People sit around the fire, and from time to time the storyteller comes to a familiar song or refrain and everyone joins in.

> *Then listen to me now;*
> *In the proverbs of the world:*
>
> *May the young woman not sleep but wake;*
> *If she sleeps, the spindle will lie.*
> *If the spindle lies, there will be no clothes;*
> *If that happens, rumor will spread.*
>
> *May the young man not sleep but wake;*
> *If he sleeps, the arrow lies.*
> *If the arrow lies, the enemy raises its head;*
> *If the enemy raises its head, politics will be lost.*
>
> *Gungma and Gesar*
> *Are like the sky and sun and moon.*
> *They are compassion and wisdom, bow and*
> *   arrow.*
> *They are the missionaries of Buddha's*
> *   teachings.*

DOCTORS AND SHAMANS

Illness is caused by a lack of understanding.
A Ladakhi *amchi*

The Ladakhi people exude a sense of well-being, vitality, and high spirits. In terms of physique, almost everyone is trim and fit—only rarely underweight and even more rarely obese. In fact, obesity is so unusual that I once overheard a woman complaining to a doctor of "strange folds in the stomach," without having any idea what they were. Even without obvious muscle (something that has puzzled Western doctors), both men and women are extremely strong, and like many other mountain peoples, they seem to have endless stamina.

The old are active until the day they die. One morning I saw the eighty-two-year-old grandfather in the house where I lived running down a ladder from the roof. He was full of life, and we exchanged a few words about the weather. That afternoon at three o'clock he died. We found him sitting peacefully as though asleep.

Of course people do get ill; respiratory infections and digestive disorders in particular are relatively common, as are skin and eye complaints. More seriously, the extreme cold of winter produces a high infant mortality rate, especially around the time of weaning. But once those first critical years have passed, the general level of health is high.

In the traditional way of life, people experience little stress and

Although life expectancy in Ladakh is lower than in the West,
people are generally fit and active even into old age.

enjoy peace of mind. The pace of their lives is relaxed and easy. They breathe pure air, get regular and prolonged exercise, and eat whole, unrefined foods. Their bodies are not forced to accommodate materials alien to the natural world of which they are a part. The food they eat is locally grown and organic, and until recently there was virtually no environmental pollution.

According to Western theory, the typical Ladakhi diet is far from balanced, with very few fruits or green vegetables; consumption of both butter and salt is, by our standards, dangerously high. Yet few of the health problems seen in the West as consequences of such imbalance are found. Despite the extremely high cholesterol intake, for instance, heart disease has been almost nonexistent. The reasons for this are probably twofold. First, what we think of as the absolute rights and wrongs of nutrition are not so absolute, as we are gradually realizing, but are dependent on a variety of other factors: exercise, or stress, for example. Second, it seems likely that human nutritional needs have to a great extent evolved according to the nature of the environment in which people live, so that the body's requirements come to coincide with what the land itself can provide. Just as Eskimos can be healthy on a diet of fish and meat, with virtually no grain, so the Ladakhis can prosper on barley and dairy products.

Responsibility for the sick is primarily in the hands of the *amchi.* Most villages have at least one *amchi,* some many more. They are among the most respected members of the community and generally learn their craft from their fathers and grandfathers before them. They do not work full time, for like everyone else, they too farm their own land.

The Tibetan system of medicine, which has recently been gaining considerable respect in the West, dates back to the eighth century. Closely related to Buddhism, the system is very comprehensively documented. Four basic treatises *(rgyut zi)* deal in detail with anatomy, the process of life, and diagnosis and treatment of disease, whereas others give specialized information about the preparation and effects of specific drugs. One volume serves as a dictionary of medical expressions. A large proportion of the various texts is given over to the preventive role of medicine: how to look after your own health, diet during pregnancy, the care of infants.

As is common in other traditional systems of medicine, diagnosis involves an examination of the whole patient. Illness is not seen as a malfunctioning of this or that particular part of the body, but as a more general imbalance. Disorders are viewed from a broader perspective, with body, mind, and spirit recognized as integral parts of the same entity. As a consequence, a part of the prescribed cure will often be spiritually oriented—the saying of mantras or even the performance of prostrations. More so perhaps than in Western medicine, the *amchi*'s experience is all-important. His patients are his fellow villagers, so he has an intimate knowledge of their habits and character.

The chief method of diagnosis is the taking of the pulses, a highly skilled technique that requires years of practice. There are twelve pulses altogether, six on each side. I was incredulous when I first heard this. An *amchi* explained to me that what was being felt was not only the physical movement of the artery, but also the energy flows corresponding with the functioning of different organs. The *amchi* will also diagnose from the color and texture of different parts of the tongue and eyes. Facial expressions, tone of voice, as well as quickness to anger and other modes of behavior are also taken into account.

I once visited an *amchi* with a neighbor's young son whose knee was infected. The *amchi,* who seemed very capable, held the boy's wrists briefly, glanced at his tongue and eyes, and then went to the room where he kept his medical equipment. The room was a mass of books, jars, and pouches—row after row of different preparations. *Thanka*s hung from the walls, while other objects of ritual—bells, bowls of holy water, prayer wheels—lay amidst an assortment of powders, juices, rocks, and herbs. The *amchi* took down some bunches of herbs and ground them together with water and black powder from a jar, chanting a mantra as he did so. The finished remedy was a greenish black paste that he spread in an even layer on the swelling, then covered it with cloth. Within a few days, the knee was cured.

Generally, the *amchi* uses natural compounds. One of the principal medical texts describes the various minerals and plants used, where to find them, and what they look like. These remedies are administered in the form of decoctions, powders, or tablets. Decoctions are used to attack the principal symptoms and take effect rapidly. Powders and tablets, on the other hand, work more subtly and are supposed to counter the underlying causes of the disorder. Prolonged headache, for instance, might be treated with a bitter powder called *titka gatpa,* a compound of eight flowers, herbs, roots, and barks based on crushed gentian. In addition, the *amchi* will almost always recommend a special diet. Most unusual of all treatments that I have known was the one recommended by an *amchi* in Zanskar for a woman whom a Western doctor diagnosed as suffering from hepatitis. "Strong sexual intercourse" was urged upon her; remarkably, the patient was greatly improved only a few days later! Another unusual and shocking remedy is the practice of placing a hot iron directly on the skin, leaving a small scar. Ladakhis who have undergone this treatment assure me that it is effective and painless.

Surgery is not practiced. I have been told that it was outlawed centuries ago when the thirty-eighth queen of Ladakh was accidentally killed by the surgeon's knife. Stitches are not used either, even for big wounds. Instead the site is cleaned with an herbal powder, and blood coagulant tablets are administered. Fractures are immobilized with wooden splints. The need for emergency intervention is rare. Appendicitis, perforated ulcers, and most of the other sudden-onset conditions common in the West are rarely encountered. In the absence of dangerous machinery and fast cars, accidents are few and far between and are unlikely to be serious. Even such a relatively trivial injury as a broken leg is unusual.

In traditional Ladakhi society there are very few signs of neurosis. Nonetheless, they are recognized in the medical texts. An *amchi* once gave me two examples of mentally disturbed patients. One is always silent, very frightened. The other talks too much, is very aggressive, and will suddenly jump up and leave the room. The treatment, he said, involves shutting the patient up in his house with a friend, who will "tell him stories and sweet things." He had never come across either of these two conditions himself but had merely read about them in books.

In addition to the *amchi,* two other individuals in the village also provide assistance to the sick. One is the *lhaba,* or shaman; the other is the *onpo,* or astrologer. Which of the three is consulted depends both on the villager concerned and on his or her particular problem. Generally, the *amchi* will be approached first, though certain problems—infertility, for instance—might be taken to one of the other two.

The *onpo* relies on books of astrological charts. His work covers almost every aspect of village life: selecting sites for new buildings, determining the day to begin sowing and harvesting the fields, checking the auspiciousness of proposed marriage partners, naming the time for funerals. He has eight basic texts, of which one, the *gyektsis,* deals exclusively with illness. With the help of the *loto,* the annually revised book of astrological computations, he is able to diagnose and recommend cures. Typically, his remedies involve the reading of sacred books or the performance of a prayer service. Throwing dice and interpreting patterns of grain are among the other methods he uses.

In my first years in Ladakh, I helped several foreign film teams. Inevitably, they wanted to shoot a Buddhist ceremony—preferably one with a lot of dancing, masks, and costume. They wanted footage of the royal family; and they wanted to see a *lhaba* in action.

*Lhaba*s are the most spectacular of Ladakh's healers. While in a trance, they become vehicles for spirits who speak through them and perform various kinds of healing. In 1975, while I was working with a German producer, our guide arranged for us to visit a *lhaba* close to Leh who would consent to being filmed.

We left Leh early one morning with the crew and all the gear in the back of the jeep. After an hour's journey we arrived at a simple house in Thikse. The *lhaba,* whose name was Tsewang, was on the roof terrace with his wife, sorting seeds. He was wearing the traditional purple dyed robe, and his white hair was cut traditionally—shaved in front and tied in a braid at the back, highlighting a high forehead. He looked about seventy and had sparkling eyes. In our first brief conversation he showed even more than the usual Ladakhi vitality and humor. We immediately became friends.

We went down into the house, where he started preparing himself for the ritual. He washed his hands and face and arranged offerings for the altar. Ten or twelve other people were there—Ladakhis who had come for healing. In the room where the ceremony was to happen we were all a little nervous. We sat on the floor and waited. After a while the *lhaba* entered the room, wearing a five-sided crown and a cloth that concealed his face. He was carrying a *damaru*—a little hand drum with two beads attached to it by strings. Setting up a slow rhythm with the drum, he began to chant in time, rocking back and forth. I was looking at the *thanka*s on the wall and trying to remember the names of all the different Buddhas and Bodhisattvas in them when I noticed that something in the quality of his chant was affecting me. I looked around at the others in the film crew and saw that it was affecting them too. As the rhythm of the drumbeat quickened, we were all drawn in by it. I saw the producer looking a little tense. As the speed of the *lhaba*'s chanting increased, it got louder and higher, becoming hypnotic and unearthly. I started shivering, and I wasn't alone.

Suddenly the voice changed to a high-pitched shriek. "Come!" He motioned roughly to the first patient, a woman with a sick child. She moved up closer to him, and I saw that she was shaking too. The *lhaba* screeched at her, "You have been behaving badly. You have not shown reverence for the spirits; you have not kept their ceremonies and you have disturbed them. You must stop this or the child will not be well."

The second patient was a woman of seventy who had a question about her grandson's future. Should he follow in his father's footsteps and become an *amchi* or should he be sent away to study Western medicine? The *lhaba* placed his drum on a table and threw some barley into the air above it. The woman pointed to one of the grains that had landed on the drum, and the remainder were brushed off. All eyes were on the drum. Standing three feet away, the *lhaba* began a haunting chant, and the grain started to turn, slowly and mysteriously. The woman sobbed quietly as the *lhaba* gave his interpretation—her grandson should be sent away.

Our driver was sneaking a cigarette from his pocket to calm his nerves. The *lhaba* saw him, instantly leapt toward him, and lashed out at him, shouting, "Don't you know how sinful it is to smoke and that the spirits will be against you if you do?" The terrified driver twisted out of his grasp and ran outside. The film crew was very shaken now by the power and unpredictability of the *lhaba*. I wondered if he—or the spirit—might decide that filming was immoral also and throw us all out. Though not a large man, he was possessed by a tremendous energy.

Now a queue of kneeling people had formed at the feet of the *lhaba*. A man with a chest infection was next in line. The *lhaba* lunged at him, tore open his robe, and buried his head in the man's chest. He raised his head and then spat out a black liquid into a bowl that his wife held out for him.

"What is he doing?" the producer asked our guide.

"It is the disease. The *lhaba* sucks the illness from the patient's body."

One by one people moved up to offer themselves to the *lhaba*. He would scream at them, push them, give them mantras or grains of rice charged with power. He sucked at their bodies, again and again spitting black fluid into the bowl.

The camera crew was filming the wild events going on around them as well as they could, but they were finding it difficult. The intensity of the *lhaba* was hard to bear. When the last patient had been shoved and shouted at, the *lhaba* spun around, faced the altar in the corner of the room, and began to chant again in the same high-pitched voice. He bowed to the altar and then suddenly slumped to the floor in silence. The ceremony was over. The *lhaba* was once again the man we had met on the roof, though tired. I stood up with difficulty, thanked him, and then joined the others outside.

"Did you understand what he said?" one of the crew asked me.

"Not much. A lot of it wasn't Ladakhi at all, I think."

"People in this village say that the spirit is Tibetan," our guide explained, "so that when the *lhaba* is possessed, he speaks Tibetan."

We walked back to the jeep in silence. It had been a very moving encounter that none of us had expected. We were not sure how to deal with it.

CHAPTER FOUR

WE HAVE TO LIVE TOGETHER

*Even a man with a hundred horses may need to ask another
for a whip.*

Ladakhi saying

"**W**hy can't you give us a room? We'll pay a reasonable price."

Angchuk and Dolma looked down, indicating that they were not going to change their minds. "You talk to Ngawang," they repeated.

"But we're already renting rooms from him, and it's getting quite noisy. There's no reason why we should rent yet another one from him."

"You're staying with Ngawang now, and he might be offended if we offer you a room."

"I'm sure he wouldn't be so unfair! Please go ahead and give us a room, won't you?"

"Talk to him first—we have to live together."

I was spending the summer of 1983 with a team of professors doing socioecological research in the village of Tongde in Zanskar. After a month or so, some of them felt the need for an extra room for quiet study. Since the house where we were staying was full of young and boisterous children, we thought we would ask the neighbors. At first I felt annoyed at Angchuk and Dolma's stubborn refusal. To me, with my emphasis on individual rights, this seemed so unfair. But their reaction, "We have to live together," made me think. It seemed that to the Ladakhis the overriding issue was coexistence. It was more important to keep good relations with your neighbor than to earn some money.

Another time, Sonam and his neighbor had asked the carpenter to make some window frames; they were both building extensions to their houses. When the carpenter was finished, he brought all the frames to the neighbor. A few days later, I went with Sonam to collect them. Some were missing; his neighbor had used more than he had ordered. This was a considerable inconvenience to Sonam since he could do no further construction work until the frames were in place, and it was going to take several weeks to have new ones made. Yet he showed no signs of resentment or anger. When I suggested to him that his neighbor had behaved badly, he simply said, "Maybe he needed them more urgently than I did." "Aren't you going to ask for an explanation?" I asked. Sonam just smiled and shrugged his shoulders: "*Chi choen?* ("What's the point?") Anyway, we have to live together."

A concern not to offend or upset one another is deeply rooted in Ladakhi society; people avoid situations that might lead to friction or conflict. When someone transgresses this unwritten law, as in the case of Sonam's neighbor, extreme tolerance is the response. And yet concern for community does not have the oppressive effect on the individual that one might have imagined. On the contrary, I am now convinced that being a part of a close-knit community provides a profound sense of security.

In traditional Ladakh, aggression of any sort is exceptionally rare: rare enough to say that it is virtually nonexistent. If you ask a Ladakhi to tell you about the last fight he can remember, you are likely to get mischievous answers like "I'm always beating up my neighbor. Only yesterday, I tied him to a tree and cut both his ears off." Should you get a serious answer, you will be told that there has been no fighting in the village in living memory. Even arguments are rare. I have hardly ever seen anything more than mild disagreement in the traditional villages—certainly nothing compared with what you find in the West. Do the Ladakhis conceal or repress their feelings?

I asked Sonam once, "Don't you have arguments? We do in the West all the time."

He thought for a minute. "Not in the villages, no—well, very very seldom, anyway."

"How do you manage it?" I asked.

He laughed. "What a funny question. We just live with each other, that's all."

"So what happens if two people disagree—say, about the boundaries of their land?"

"They'll talk about it, of course, and discuss it. What would you expect them to do?"

I didn't reply.

One means of ensuring a lack of friction in traditional Ladakhi society is something I call the "spontaneous intermediary." As soon as any sort of difference arises between two parties, a third party is there to act as arbiter. Whatever the circumstances, whoever is involved, an intermediary always seems to be on hand. It happens automatically, without any prompting; the intermediary is not consciously sought and can be anyone who happens to be around; it might be an older sister, or a neighbor, or just a passing stranger. I have seen the process function even with young children. I remember watching a five-year-old settling a squabble between two of his friends in this way. They listened to him willingly. The feeling that peace is better than conflict is so deeply ingrained that people turn automatically to a third party.

This mechanism prevents problems from arising in the first place. The spontaneous intermediary, it seems, is always around in any context that might possibly lead to conflict. If two people are involved in trade, for example, they can be sure that someone will be there to help them strike a deal. This way they avoid the possibility of direct confrontation. In most situations, the parties already know one another. But if someone unknown to the others intervenes, it is not seen as meddling—the help will be welcomed.

One spring I was traveling on a truck from Kargil to Zanskar. Since snow still covered the road, the journey was taking longer than usual, but though it was rough and uncomfortable, I was enjoying the experience. It was fascinating observing our driver. He was exceptionally large and burly for a Ladakhi and had become a bit of a hero in the short time since the road had been built. Everywhere along the way, people knew him. Traveling up and down the road every few weeks, he had become an important personage in the eyes of the villagers—sending messages, delivering parcels, and carrying passengers.

He had brought a sack of rice, for which he wanted some of the famous creamy Zanskari butter. As he approached an old woman, a large crowd gathered around. Suddenly a young boy no more than twelve years old was taking charge. He was telling this King of the Road how much to expect, what was reasonable. The whole affair lasted fifteen minutes, the driver and the old woman bartering through the young lad, never directly with each other. It seemed incongruous, this big tough man meekly following the advice of a boy half his size, yet so appropriate.

Traditional Ladakhi villages are run democratically, and, with few exceptions, every family owns its own land. Disparities in wealth are minimal. About 95 percent of the population belongs to what one might call a middle class. The remainder is split more or less evenly between an aristocracy and a lower class. This latter group is made up primarily of Mons, the early settlers of Ladakh, who are usually carpenters and blacksmiths. Their low status is attributed to the fact that extracting metals from the earth is thought to anger the spirits. Differences between these three classes exist, but they do not give rise to social tension. In contrast to European social boundaries, the classes interact on a day-to-day basis. It would not be unusual to see a Mon, for instance, joking with a member of the royal family.

Since every farmer is almost completely self-sufficient, and thus largely independent, there is little need for communal decision making; each household essentially works its own land with its own resources. Many activities that would otherwise require the whole village to sit down and draw up plans—like the painting of the village monastery or arrangements for Losar (New Year)—have been worked out many generations ago and are now done by rotation. Nonetheless, sometimes matters have to be decided on a village level. Larger villages are divided up into *chutsos*, or groups of ten houses, each of which has at least one representative on the village council.

This body meets periodically throughout the year and is presided over by the *goba,* or village head.

The *goba* is usually appointed by rotation. If the whole village wants to keep him on, he may hold his position for many years, but otherwise after a year or so, the job will pass on to another householder. One of the *goba's* jobs is to act as adjudicator. Though arguments are unusual, from time to time some differences of opinion arise that need settling.

Visiting the *goba* is a relaxed occasion, with little formality. Often the parties involved sit in the kitchen and discuss the problem together with the help of a little tea or *chang.* I have spent a lot of time in the house of Paljor, the *goba* in the village of Tongde, listening as he helped to settle disputes. Since my research in Tongde focused on child-rearing practices, I would often sit in the kitchen with Paljor's wife, Tsering, who had just had a baby. People would come in from time to time to talk to Paljor.

Once two villagers, Namgyal and Chospel, came to the house with a problem. Namgyal started telling us what had happened: "My horse, Rompo, got loose this morning. I had tied her to a big stone while I went in to talk to Norbu about his broken plough. I don't know how she got loose, but somehow she did." "I saw her from my rooftop," Chospel continued. "She was munching away at my barley; she had already chewed off a whole corner of the field. I threw a stone to scare her off, but then I saw her fall; I must have hurt her."

Throwing stones, often with a yak-hair sling, is the way in which Ladakhis usually keep their animals under control, and they can throw with astonishing accuracy. I have seen them control whole flocks of sheep nearly half a mile away with a few deftly placed stones. But this time, Chospel's aim had been off, and he had hit the horse just below the knee, injuring her leg.

Who should compensate whom? And for how much? Although the horse's injury was more serious than the loss of the barley, Namgyal was guilty of an offense that could not be overlooked. To protect their crops, Ladakhis have agreed on strict rules about stray animals, and each village has someone, called a *lorapa,* specially appointed to catch them and collect a fine from the owner. After much discussion, the three men decided that no compensation was necessary either way. As Paljor told Namgyal: "Hurting Rompo's leg was an accident, and you were careless in letting her go loose."

Before coming to Ladakh, I had always thought that the best judges were the ones who were in no way connected with the individuals they were judging; maintaining this neutrality and distance, it seemed, was the only way of administering real justice. Perhaps it is, when you are talking about a society on the scale of our own. But having lived in Ladakh for many years, I have had to change my mind. Though no system of justice can be perfect, none is more effective than one that is based on small, close-knit communities and that allows people to settle their problems at a grass-roots level, by discussion among themselves. I have learned that when the people settling disputes are intimately acquainted with the parties involved, their judgment is not prejudiced; on the contrary, this very closeness helps them to make fairer and sounder decisions. Not only do smaller units allow for a more human form of justice, they also help prevent the sort of conflict that is so much a part of larger communities.

In fact, the more time I spent in Ladakh, the more I came to realize the importance of scale. At first, I sought to explain the Ladakhis' laughter and absence of anger or stress in terms of their values and religion. These did, no doubt, play an important role. But gradually I became aware that the external structures shaping the society, scale in particular, were just as important. They had a profound effect on the individual and in turn reinforced his or her beliefs and values.

Since villages are rarely larger than a hundred houses, the scale of life is such that people can directly experience their mutual interdependence. They have an overview and can comprehend the structures and networks of which they are a part, seeing the effects of their actions and thus feeling a sense of responsibility. And because their actions are more visible to others, they are more easily held accountable.

Economic and political interactions are almost always face to face; buyer and seller have a personal connection, a connection that discourages carelessness or deceit. As a result, corruption or abuse of power is very rare. Smaller scale also limits the amount of power vested in one individual. What a difference between the president of a nation-state and the *goba* in a Ladakhi village: one has power over several millions of people whom he will never meet and who will never have the opportunity to speak to him; the other coordinates the affairs of a few hundred people whom he knows intimately, and who interact with him on a daily basis.

In the traditional Ladakhi village, people have much control over their own lives. To a very great extent they make their own decisions rather than being at the mercy of faraway, inflexible bureaucracies and fluctuating markets. The human scale allows for spontaneous decision making and action based on the needs of the particular context. There is no need for rigid legislation; instead, each situation brings forth a new response.

Ladakhis have been fortunate enough to inherit a society in which the good of the individual is not in conflict with that of the whole community; one person's gain is not another person's loss. From family and neighbors to members of other villages and even strangers, Ladakhis are aware that helping others is in their own interest. A high yield for one farmer does not entail a low yield for another. Mutual aid, rather than competition, shapes the economy. It is, in other words, a synergistic society.

Cooperation is formalized in a number of social institutions. Among the most important is the *paspun*. Every family in the village belongs to a group of households that helps each other out at the time of birth, marriage, and death. The group consists of between four and twelve households, sometimes from different villages. Generally they share the same household god, who is believed to protect the families from harm and disease. At New Year, offerings are made to the god at a small shrine on the roof of each house. The *paspun* is most active at the time of a funeral. After death, the body is kept in the family house until the day of cremation (usually a week or so later), but the family does not need to touch it. The *paspun* members have the responsibility to wash and prepare the body; from the moment of death until the body has been totally consumed by fire, it is they who arrange most of the work so that the relatives are spared unnecessary distress.

A monk comes to read from the *Bardo Thodol,* the Tibetan *Book of the Dead,* for the period before the funeral. The consciousness of the dead person is told of experiences in the afterlife and urged not to be afraid of demons but to turn instead toward the pure white light, the "clear light of the void."

On the day of the cremation, hundreds of people gather at the house, bringing the customary gifts of bread and barley flour. The relatives of the deceased, in particular the women, sit in the kitchen wailing the mourning chant over and over between tears: "*Tussi loma, tussi loma . . .*" ("Like falling autumn leaves, the leaves of time"). Neighbors and friends file past, expressing sympathy: "*Tserka macho*" ("Don't be sad"). The sounds of the monks' music and chanting fill the house.

The first funeral I attended was in the village of Stok, when a friend's grandfather died. Just after midday we were served a meal. The *paspun* members were in a sense acting as hosts. When they were not stirring the giant thirty-gallon pots of butter tea, we could see them dashing around with plates of food in their hands, making sure everyone was served. In the early afternoon, while the women stayed behind at the house, the monks led the funeral procession to the cremation site. Wearing brightly colored brocade and tall headdresses with thick black fringes hanging down over their eyes, they emerged from the chapel with a great flurry of drums and shawms. They walked slowly through the fields toward the edge of the village. Behind them came the *paspun:* four men carrying the body on a litter with the others bringing wood for the fire. After them followed a long line of male friends and relatives. As the monks performed the "burning of offerings" beside the small clay oven, the *paspun* alone remained with them, tending the fire.

The *paspun,* just like the *chutso,* brings a sense of belonging to an intimate group that remains together for life, united by a common purpose. In traditional Ladakhi society, people have special links not only with their own family and immediate neighbors, but with households scattered throughout the entire region as well.

Again, human scale allows for flexibility. If, for instance, a *paspun* member happens to be in the middle of the harvest or some other crucial work when a funeral is to take place, no unbending rule says that he must drop his work and go. If he cannot be there, he may talk with other *paspun* members and make arrangements for someone else to take his place.

Much farming work is shared, either by the whole community or by smaller subgroups like the *chutso*. During the harvest, for instance, farmers help one another to gather their crops. This works well since fields ripen at different times even in the same village. With everyone working together, the harvest can be gathered in quickly as soon as it is ripe.

Bes, as shared work of this sort is called, often incorporates more than one village, and the reasons for it are not always purely economic. Some farmers will stagger the harvest, even when two fields are ripe at the same time, just so they can work together. You almost never see people harvesting alone; instead, you find groups of men, women, and children all together in the fields—always with constant laughter and song.

Rares (literally, "goat turn") is the communal shepherding of animals. It is not necessary for someone from each household to go up to the mountains with the animals every single day; instead one or two people take all the sheep and goats from several households and leave everyone else free to do other work.

Private property is also shared. The small stone houses up at the *phu,* though owned by one household, will be used by many, usually in exchange for some work, or milk or cheese. In the same way, the water mills used for grinding grain are available to everyone. If you do not own one yourself, you can make arrangements to use someone else's; and only in late autumn, when the water is very scarce and everyone is trying to grind as much grain as possible for winter, might you compensate the owner with some of the ground flour.

At the busiest times of the agricultural year, farm tools and draft animals are shared. Especially at the time of sowing—when the earth is finally ready after the long winter and farmers must work hard to

A young shepherd girl at Nyimaling phu, 16,000 feet above sea level. Children learn to take responsibility at an early age.

prepare the fields—families pool their resources to enable everything to be done as quickly as possible. Again, this practice is sufficiently formalized to have a name, *lhangsde,* but within this formal structure, too, a high degree of flexibility is possible.

Once I was in the village of Sakti at sowing time. Two households had an arrangement whereby they shared animals, plough, and labor for the few days before sowing could start. Their neighbor, Sonam Tsering, who was not a part of the group, was ploughing his own fields when one of his *dzo* sat down and refused to work any longer. I thought at first that it was just being stubborn, but Tsering told me that the animal was ill and that he feared it was serious. Just as we were sitting at the edge of the field wondering what to do, the farmer from next door came by and without a moment's hesitation offered his own help as well as the help of the others in his *lhangsde* group. That evening, after they had finished their own work, they all came over to Tsering's fields with their *dzo.* As always, they sang as they worked; and long after dark, when I could no longer see them, I could still hear their song.

CHAPTER FIVE

AN UNCHOREOGRAPHED DANCE

*"The Ladakhi lady is complete head of her own household, and
the men are well underneath her capable thumb. She has her own
money, she trades on her own; her word is very much law."*

Major M. L. A. Gompertz, *Magic Ladakh,* 1928

Dolma was twenty-five when she married Angchuk, who was two
years younger. She came from Shadi, a tiny village upstream from
Tongde, nestled high up in the mountains. The two villages have a lot
of contact with each other. A very high percentage of marriage partners in Tongde come from Shadi, and because Tongde, at a lower altitude, has more grain and Shadi, higher up, more animals, the
villages trade between themselves as well.

Dolma's marriage, like others in Ladakh, is polyandrous. She is
also married to Angchuk's younger brother, Angdus. However, the
third brother remains celibate—a monk in Tongde Monastery. I have
heard of some cases in which the third brother joined the marriage,
but this is rare.

As Angchuk is the oldest brother, he is the head of the household
and the senior husband. He is the "boss," but the hierarchy is not very
rigid, and in most situations it would be difficult to tell that he is.
Dolma treats her husbands more or less the same; she refers to both
of them as *atcho,* or "elder brother," and does not seem to favor one or
the other.

When I was in Tongde, I visited them often and got to know

Dolma well. We would sit together for hours, discussing differences between life in Zanskar and the West. The emotional side of polyandry fascinated me. How did it feel having more than one husband? I asked her whether she loved one brother more than the other. She was embarrassed at first because affection between husband and wife is not expressed openly. Rarely will you see couples holding hands; you will never see them kissing.

"Angdus is more gentle, but I am close to them both," she said shyly. If she did not use the verb *love,* it is because Ladakhi has no word to express our Western preoccupation with an exclusive, passionate, romantic attachment.

When I talked to Angdus and Angchuk about their relationship with Dolma, they seemed a bit embarrassed too, especially when the discussion turned to sex. They took turns sleeping with Dolma, they told me, though Angchuk would sleep with her more often as Angdus spent a lot of time on trading trips; but sometimes—and it was said with such howls of laughter that I did not know whether to believe it—they would all three sleep together, with Dolma in the middle.

Even though Ladakhis are reluctant to show affection in public, they are far from sexually inactive; they seem neither repressed nor promiscuous. Extramarital sex is discouraged, but the attitude is more "These things will happen." Mothers of illegitimate children are not outcasts. In fact, losing your temper is more scorned than being unfaithful. One of the strongest insults you can hurl at a Ladakhi is *schon chan,* "one who angers easily." Angchuk Dawa, a student who has helped me translate folktales, explained that it is bad form for a cuckolded husband to make a scene. "You see, if he should become enraged and kick up a terrible fuss, it would be *his* conduct, rather than hers, that would be judged more harshly."

Polyandry has been a key factor in maintaining a relatively stable population in Ladakh over the centuries. This stability has in turn, I believe, contributed to the environmental balance and social harmony. That population control is an important factor in maintaining a balance with the environment is clear. The link with social harmony is perhaps less so. Nevertheless, it seems that social friction is likely to be reduced if the number of people depending on a fixed quantity of resources remains the same from generation to generation. Under those circumstances, the need for scrambling and fighting to survive is clearly minimized.

The ratio of men to women in Ladakh is roughly equal, so if a number of men take one wife, it means that some women do not marry. Fewer married women means fewer children. Women who do not marry become nuns. And, in fact, a large number of men, usually one or more of the younger brothers, also remain unmarried, living as monks. Thus polyandry has worked hand in hand with the monasticism of Tibetan Buddhism.

Technically illegal since 1942, polyandry was much less common when I arrived than it had been in days gone by. To what extent it had decreased is difficult to judge; it is not clear how prevalent it was in its heyday. However, it was certainly common enough to have a considerable effect in keeping the population down.

Interestingly enough, though polyandry is the preferred form of marriage, it is not the only one. There is some polygamy and monogamy as well. This unusual situation probably reflects a careful adaptation to scarce resources. By keeping social relationships so flexible, the relationship to the land can remain optimal. In other words, from one generation to another, each family has the freedom to choose the ideal marriage option, depending on the amount of land available, the number of offspring and potential partners, and so on.

Polygamous marriages often occur when a woman cannot bear children. In those circumstances, a second wife, usually her sister, marries into the family. However there can be other reasons too. In the case of Deskit and Angmo, whom I came to know in Zanskar, the situation was rather different. Not only were these two unrelated, but Deskit had had several children with her husband, Namgyal, before Angmo appeared. Namgyal had been having an affair with Angmo. When she got pregnant, he told Deskit that he would like to bring her and the baby into their home and to treat her as a second wife.

I asked Deskit how she had felt, whether she had liked the idea of having Angmo in the house. "I didn't," she said. "I didn't like the idea at all at first. I was upset. But Namgyal and Angmo were so keen that we should all live together that I thought, *"Chi choen?*—(What's the point?) We might as well all be happy." And for twelve years now, they have been living together peacefully. According to Angmo, Deskit was friendly to her from the start. "We've never argued," she told me. "Once in a while, we get a bit annoyed with Namgyal—he can sometimes be lazy, and we have to push him to work; but the two of us, we've never fought in twelve years."

In traditional Ladakhi society, women have a very strong position, so Deskit's acceptance of Angmo had nothing to do with being downtrodden. In fact, just next door in a polyandrous marriage, the situation was the other way round. There, Norbu and his younger brother Tsewang had one wife, Palmo. Tsewang had a shop in Leh and spent a lot of time away from Tongde. But when he came back home, Norbu would often throw a party for him, and Palmo and Tsewang would sleep together.

Whatever the system of marriage, landholdings are kept intact. The guiding principle behind the system of land inheritance is that it remains undivided instead of being split into smaller and smaller pieces. Whatever happens, whatever the configuration of children may be, the land is passed on to just one individual. This is the case even when there are no children at all: then, someone is adopted as heir.

It is usually the eldest son who formally inherits the family's hold-ings. Since land is neither sold nor bought, and private ownership of land does not exist as in the West, he does not become the owner of the land, but rather a sort of guardian. If there are no sons at home, or if other circumstances make it desirable, the eldest daughter inherits everything and brings in a *magpa,* a husband who himself has no prop-erty rights.

Angchuk's situation is quite typical. The property is officially his; he inherited it at the time of his marriage. His parents, as is common custom, then moved out of the main house into a smaller cottage, or *khangu,* next door. So at an early age Angchuk became the head—and the political representative—of the household. While his grandmother and one uncle have remained in the main house, his parents are in the *khangu* with his grandfather and two of his sisters, both nuns. There are separate fields attached to the *khangu,* which they work largely for themselves, and they cook in their own kitchen. Although there is constant cooperation and the family spends a lot of time together, the two households retain a good deal of independence from one another.

Weddings almost invariably occur in winter, when there is more time for celebration. Parents, friends, and relatives all play a role in finding a suitable partner. Suggested pairings are reviewed by the *onpo* (astrologer), who decides whether the couple is astrologically matched. If he gives his approval, the groom's family begins a long series of courting rituals. Presents and pots of *chang* are sent to the family of the other side, and a friend or relative—often the maternal grandfather —is sent to sound them out. If the gifts are accepted, a number of relatives are invited to the respective houses to arrange the wedding details. Friends, family, and members of the *paspun* divide the tasks among themselves. Finally, the *onpo* decides the date of the marriage.

On the day before the wedding, a group of men who are to take the bride from her home assemble at the groom's house. They should be good singers and dancers. On the wedding day, they wear long coats of silk and tall pointed hats. That evening they arrive at the house of the bride, each carrying an arrow *(dadar)* and a small piece of ankle bone from a sheep or a goat. The arrow symbolizes the god of the house where the bride will live, the small bone, or *yangmol,* prosperity. The house is now full of guests drinking tea and *chang.* The bride has to be almost forced away by the men who stand shouting for her outside the door. Eventually she comes out, ritual tears pouring.

The most extraordinary wedding I have ever seen took place in Mangyu, a village tucked away in a valley one day's journey from Leh. Over three hundred guests celebrated the event with three days and nights of intense revelry. Then, on the fourth day, they assembled to watch the bridegroom, Tsering Wangyal, undergo a stringent examination to become an *amchi.* The art of the *amchi* is almost always passed down from father to son, with no formal testing required. But

A wedding party. Celebrations typically last many days, even weeks.

Wangyal's father, who had died three years earlier, had not been a doctor. "You are very lucky," Tashi Rabgyas told me. "Such ceremonies are extremely rare. Perhaps only eight, ten at the most, will be held this century."

The bride arrived looking nervous. For the first time in her life, her head was adorned with a turquoise-studded *perak,* which flowed down below her shoulders. By custom, a mother hands her *perak* down to her eldest daughter when she marries. That this storehouse of family wealth remains the wife's possession is an indication of the strong position women have traditionally held in Ladakhi society.

The *natitpa* (best man) and his ushers escorted her the four hundred yards or so to the house, stopping four times to make ritual toasts and dance solemnly around vessels of *chang.* Wangyal's brother, Dorje, threw coins and banknotes into the air, and children chased after them in a mad scramble. Nearer the house, a monk broke a clay pot to ward off evil spirits. The smaller the fragments, the more prosperous would be the marriage.

Most of the ceremony took place outside on the harvested fields, which had a thin cover of frost. Festivities began at three o'clock, not long after the sun had dropped behind the high mountain to the south, and continued until after nine o'clock in the evening. We sat on carpets set out in two parallel lines, facing twelve enormous pots filled with *chang*. Ladakhi hospitality being what it is, we never had to wait long for our cups to be refilled. Yet it was so cold that by the time someone brought me more, a thin layer of ice had already formed on top of the *chang*.

I took my turn presenting the bride, groom, and family with *kataks*, white scarves that are the traditional way of wishing people well. When the pile got too high around the recipient's neck, dangerously close to a hundred, a helper stood ready behind to take half of it away. The best man started off the dancing by placing a *katak* around the neck of one of the guests, and eventually nearly everyone joined in the slow, stately Ladakhi dances, always performed in a circle, which after a time have an almost hypnotic effect.

At night, the merrymaking became more riotous. A procession of dancers moved slowly and unsteadily down a narrow path cleared for them, the leader proclaiming, "I'm so drunk!" At one o'clock, Tashi Rabgyas retired discreetly to his room to sleep. An hour and a half later, the *chang* drinkers went crashing through the seclusion of his dreams, calling, "Come, Tashi! Wake up! Even scholars must sing and dance!" Fortunately for us all, *chang* tends to be merciful when it comes to hangovers.

I was amazed by the apparent ease and grace with which Wangyal's family met the needs of their three hundred houseguests. In the morning, they provided everyone with hot water, soap, and a towel (their house, of course, had no running water); hot water was also provided before every meal. The family and members of the *paspun* worked around the clock in relays preparing food. Breakfast was simple: *khambhir* (whole-grained bread) and butter tea. By the end of the fourth day, the massive mountains of butter and *khambhir* I had spied in the kitchen upon arrival had shrunk to almost nothing. Lunch and dinner were substantial: rice, cooked in enormous cauldrons, vegetables, and meat. Nobody seemed to be masterminding this carefully orchestrated hospitality, but if so much as a candle burned out, someone was always right there to replace it.

Wangyal was unflappable during the ceremonies, which were far less rigid and formal than our weddings. I was never aware of any specific moment when he and his bride became husband and wife. Perhaps it was when they sat side by side on a carpet on which two swastikas, ancient symbols of good luck, had been fashioned from barley, and together they both ate from the same plate.

Wangyal was equally unruffled on the fourth day, facing a panel of eight august *amchis*. First, he recited from memory for about forty minutes from a venerable *amchi* text. Then, with black and white pebbles, he drew on a carpet a diagram resembling a tree of life. It depicted the parts of the body and linked them with interconnecting lines to the ailments to which they fall prey. Next, the panel chose a boy at random from the crowd. Wangyal took his pulse— six different pulses from each wrist—and diagnosed the boy's physical condition, which the older *amchis* verified. Finally, they fired questions at him and, when he answered correctly, accepted him as one of them.

The majority of births occur in the warmer months of summer. For one whole week after his baby has been born, the father avoids working in the fields, for fear of inadvertently harming even the smallest insect, and thus disturbing the *lhu*. Mother and child remain peacefully in a separate room, protected from the outside world. The family spoils them, bringing the freshest and richest milk, and the best yak butter. They hang an arrow of good fortune from the willow-ribbed ceiling.

So long as the *onpo* gives his approval, it is on the seventh day that neighbors and friends are invited to see the newborn child for the first time. They come with heaped plates of flour and butter, and little figures molded from dough in the shape of an ibex, the Horse of the Gods.

In the prayer room, monks burn incense. The house echoes to the hypnotic sounds of plainsong chant, and the harsh, reedy tones of the religious music. Children chase each other in play, while their parents chatter, the merrymaking mingling with the heavy beat of the ceremonial drum.

The celebrations that take place a month after the birth involve the whole village. A child has been born to the community. The black-smith comes with gifts of a spoon and a bracelet. The musicians play a *lharnga*. *Kataks* and special food are brought for the mother and child.

The *onpo* also chooses the day on which the baby should leave the house for the first time. Nothing is left to chance. All the omens must be favorable and the elements especially well matched.

The parents rub a little butter on the baby's head for good luck, and paint a black mark of soot and oil, *jur,* on the forehead, to ward off evil spirits. They dress it in a long homespun robe and a woolen hat adorned with a silver *om.*

After two or three months, the baby is taken to the monastery to be blessed and given a printed prayer for protection. It is at this time too that the infant receives what we would consider first names from a *rinpoche,* or high lama. The names are derived from Buddhist concepts; for example, "Angchuk" and "Wangyal" mean "powerful" and "victorious" in the sense of overcoming one's ego. There is no last name as we know it. In Ladakh you are identified by the name of your house and landholding, a clear indication of a deep and lasting connection to the land.

Dolma's children refer to both Angchuk and Angdus as "abba," or "father," but any man old enough to be your father can be addressed in this way. Dolma says she knows who the father of each child is. The eldest child belongs to Angchuk, she says, the youngest one to Angdus. "How do you know?" "I just know." Neither Angdus nor Angchuk is concerned about which child is his own: the children are cared for equally.

Spending time with Dolma's family, I saw something of how children are brought up. They have continual physical contact with others, a factor that plays an important role in their development. Dolma spent more time with little Angchuk, who was six months old, than anyone else did. All night he would sleep in her arms, able to feed whenever he wanted. In the daytime she would usually take him with her if she was working in the fields. But caring for the baby was not her job alone. Everyone looked after him. Someone was always there to kiss and cuddle him. Men and women alike adore little children, and even the teenage boys from next door were not embarrassed to be seen cooing over little Angchuk or rocking him to sleep with a lullaby:

> *Alo - lo - lo . . .*
> *Alo - lo - lo . . .*
> Please give a happy sleep to our little one!
> *Alo - lo - lo . . .*

The traditional way of life allows mothers and children to remain together at all times. When villagers gather to discuss important issues, or at festivals and parties, children of all ages are always present. Even at social gatherings that run late into the night with drinking, singing, dancing, and loud music, young children can be seen running around, joining in the festivities until they simply drop off to sleep. No one tells them, "It's eight-thirty. You must be off to bed."

I told Dolma how much time some babies in the West spend away from their mothers and how at night they might sleep in another room and be fed cow's milk from plastic bottles on a schedule rather than when they cry. She was horrified: "Please, *atche* Helena, when you have children, whatever you do, don't treat your baby like that. If you want a happy baby, do like we do."

Everyone remains calm with children, even when the young ones are being demanding. Once I was working with Yeshe, a traditional doctor, translating a text on childbirth from one of his old medical books, while he was looking after his neighbor's grandson for the day. The boy kept grabbing at the pages, sometimes actually tearing them, and all the time asking, *"Chi inok? Chi inok?"* ("What's this? What's this?") He never stopped; he kept asking the same question over and over again. It was almost impossible to concentrate on what we were trying to do, but Yeshe was infinitely patient. Each time the boy got hold of the book, he would gently take his hand away, answering, "It's a book. . . it's a book. . . it's a book." He must have said it a hundred times, always in the same calm way, and unlike me, he had no trouble concentrating on our work!

Dolma once slapped her three-year-old son as he tried to grab the hot teapot. At the same moment, almost instantly, she gave him a big

Deskit, from Tongde, bathing her little boy. After drying him, she rubs melted butter all over his body, to protect him against the dryness and cold.

hug. I wondered whether receiving such unclear signals would be confusing for the child. But after I had observed many similar incidents, I realized that the message was, "I love you, but don't do that." Dolma had been demonstrating her displeasure with the act, not with her child.

Children receive unlimited and unconditional affection from everyone around them. In the West, we would say they were being "spoiled," but in fact very soon, by the time they are five or so, Ladakhi children have learned to take responsibility for someone else, carrying infants on their backs as soon as they are strong enough. Children are never segregated into peer groups; they grow up surrounded by people of all ages, from young babies to great-grandparents. They grow up as part of a whole chain of relationships, a chain of giving and taking.

Quite unprompted, a young child will break a biscuit into tiny fragments to share it with siblings or friends. This is natural and spontaneous behavior, not a conscious gesture of generosity. Countless times over the years, sticky little fingers have pressed apricots, peas, and bits of bread into my hands. At a party to celebrate the Skangsol festival, I watched two young boys, no more than ten years old, as they were given their share of the special feast—a plate that they were to share, piled high with rice, a helping of vegetables, and a piece of meat. They set about it eagerly, their nimble fingers working away at the rice, which soon disappeared. My curiosity grew as the boys paused to wipe their mouths, leaving the prized piece of meat sitting on the empty plate. Each then refused it, in typical Ladakhi fashion, insisting that the other should take it, even pushing the plate away in feigned disinterest.

Taking responsibility for other children as you yourself grow up must have a profound effect on your development. For boys in particular, it is important since it brings out their ability for caring and nurturing. In traditional Ladakh, masculine identity is not threatened by such qualities; on the contrary, it actually embraces them.

Roles are generally not so clearly defined as they are in the West. The vast majority of people are not specialists; instead, they have learned a whole range of skills to provide for their needs. With the exception of a very few tasks that are the exclusive province of either men or women—like ploughing the fields, which only men do—almost all activities are carried out on an unstructured basis; most work within the family or village is done in a relaxed, spontaneous way by either sex.

While in Tongde, I tried for a long time to figure out how work was coordinated. Things seemed to get done without the need for discussion and there appeared to be no regular pattern. Sitting in Angchuk and Dolma's kitchen was like watching an unchoreographed dance. No one said, "You do this," "Shall I do that?" Yet, smoothly and gracefully, everything that needed doing got done. One minute Uncle Dawa was cuddling the baby, the next he was stirring a pot on the stove, then he was bringing in some flour from the larder. He passed little Angchuk to Dolma, who held him on her lap as she chopped vegetables. Angchuk pumped the bellows to keep the fire burning and held out a pot for Uncle Dawa to pour the flour into. Abi-le, or Grandmother, took over at the stove while Angdus began to mold the dough for bread. Dolma went out to fetch water from the stream that ran beside the house. Then Uncle Dawa sat down beside the stove. He spun his prayer wheel of shining copper and brass while gently murmuring a sacred mantra, as if it were an accompaniment to the movement around him.

Old people participate in all spheres of life. For the elderly in Ladakh, there are no years of staring into space, unwanted and alone; they are important members of the community until the day they die. Old age implies years of valuable experience and wisdom. Grandparents are not so strong, but they have other qualities to contribute; there is no hurry to life, so if they work more slowly it does not matter. They remain a part of the family and community, so active that even in their eighties they are usually fit and healthy, their minds clear.

One of the main reasons old people remain so alive and involved is their constant contact with the young. The relationship between grandparent and child is different from that between parent and child. The very oldest and the very youngest form a special bond; they are often best friends.

In Dolma's family, the children would inevitably run to Grandmother for consolation if they had been hurt or reprimanded. She would rock them or play with them until all was forgotten. It was Abi-le who would ask special favors on their behalf, and it was she who made tiny ibex figures out of cheese for them, stringing them into a necklace that they could nibble on.

As I write this, another such scene is being played out in front of me. Outside the window, two maroon-colored shapes are moving slowly toward me between the fields of barley. The path is stony and steep, and as they come closer, I can see that a little boy monk is helping an older one. Bent and shaking slightly, the old man, perhaps eighty years of age, hesitates at every boulder and turn. The little shape zigzags back and forth, finding the best position from which to give a helping hand.

One of the first things that struck me on my arrival in Ladakh was the wide, uninhibited smiles of the women, who moved about freely, joking and speaking with men in an open and unselfconscious way. Though young girls may sometimes appear shy, women generally exhibit great self-confidence, strength of character, and dignity. Almost all early travelers to Ladakh commented on the exceptionally strong position of women.

Anthropologists looking from a Western perspective at formal, external structures might get a misleading impression, since men tend to hold the public positions and often sit separately from women at social functions. However, from my experience of several industrial societies, I would say that women in Ladakh actually have a stronger position than in any other culture I know. Once I understood the society more from the inside, as it were, I became aware that differences in roles did not necessarily mean inequality. I sensed a dynamic balance; it was difficult to say who had more real power, men or women. When Dolma sat with her female friends at a party, chatting away, there was no question of sexual discrimination. And although differences between the sexes are not denied in Ladakh, in some ways they are less accentuated than they are in the West. For instance, names for men and women are often identical, and the one pronoun *kho* stands for both "he" and "she."

"I don't want to get married and have children. I would rather become a nun," a Ladakhi friend once said to me. In some cases, women with children choose to leave their families to become nuns; and there are nuns who choose to marry, as well as those who have "illegitimate" children. The role of the nun is surprisingly flexible and rather unusual. Most nuns live at home. In appearance they can be distinguished by their short hair, and they spend more time in prayer than the rest of the family. They benefit from close-knit family and community ties. Even though they remain celibate, they are involved in caring for the young, so they too have close contact with children.

Undoubtedly, monks rank higher than nuns in the formal hierarchy, yet the balance between male and female plays a central role in Buddhist teachings. A monk explained, "Just like the two wings of a bird must be balanced for it to fly, so one cannot attain enlightenment unless wisdom is accompanied by compassion." The female is symbolic of wisdom, the male of compassion! Together they form the very essence of the religion.

Most significant of all for the status of women in Ladakh is the fact that the "informal" sector, with women at the center, plays a much larger role than the "formal" one. The focus of the economy is the household; almost all important decisions to do with basic needs are settled at this level. So women are never forced to choose between being with their children and playing an active part in social and economic life. As I mentioned earlier, there is little need for communal decision making. Thus the public sphere, in which men tend to be the leaders, has far less significance than in the industrialized world.

Although the difference is marginal, women on the whole work harder than men. Unlike in the West, however, they are given full recognition for everything they do. In this agrarian society, maintaining good relations with family and community is vital; so too is a knowledge of the land and animals. In these areas women excel.

I remember talking to a young woman a few months after her brother had married:

"Was it an arranged marriage?" I asked.

"Yes, my brother wanted it that way. It's very important for both families to be involved. They can bring a lot of experience and knowledge to an important decision like this."

*Women in Ladakh are strong and confident. In the traditional agrarian
economy, their work is valued as highly as that of men.*

"Are there special qualities that people look for when choosing a wife?"

"Well, first of all, she should be able to get along with people, to be fair and tolerant."

"What else is important?"

"Her skills are valued, and she shouldn't be lazy."

"Does it matter if she's pretty or not?"

"Not really. It's what she's like inside that counts—her character is more important. We say here in Ladakh, 'A tiger's stripes are on the outside; human stripes are on the inside.'"

CHAPTER SIX

BUDDHISM: A WAY OF LIFE

Know all things to be like this:
A mirage, a cloud castle,
A dream, an apparition,
Without essence, but with qualities that can be seen.

Know all things to be like this:
As the moon in a bright sky
In some clear lake reflected,
Though to that lake the moon has never moved.

Know all things to be like this:
As an echo that derives
From music, sounds, and weeping,
Yet in that echo is no melody.

Know all things to be like this:
As a magician makes illusions
Of horses, oxen, carts, and other things,
Nothing is as it appears.

Samadhirajasutra

Everything in Ladakh reflects its religious heritage. The landscape is dotted with walls of carved prayer stones and *chortens*, fluttering flags whisper prayers to the winds, and always on some distant height rise the massive white walls of a monastery. Buddhism has been the traditional religion of the majority of Ladakhis since approximately 200

B.C., when it was introduced from India. Today, all sects of Tibetan Mahayana Buddhism are represented, under the overall spiritual leadership of His Holiness the Dalai Lama.

The villages where I have lived are Buddhist, but in the capital almost half the population is Muslim. In addition, there is a small group of Christians numbering a few hundred. Relations among these three groups have changed in recent years, but when I arrived they all showed profound mutual respect and an easygoing tolerance, strengthened by quite frequent intermarriages. On the main festival days of the respective religions, people of all groups would visit one another, exchanging *kataks*, the ceremonial white scarves. In my first few months in Ladakh, I was invited to join in the festivities at the time of Id, a Muslim holiday. I will never forget the sense of warmth and good humor as Buddhists and Muslims sat down together.

One of the central elements of Buddhism is the philosophy of *sunyata*, or "emptiness." I had difficulty understanding the meaning of this concept at first, but over the years, in talking to Tashi Rabgyas, it became clearer: "It is something that is not easy to talk about, and impossible to understand through words alone," he told me once. "It is something you can only fully grasp through a combination of reflection and personal experience. But I'll try to explain it in a simple way. Take any object, like a tree. When you think of a tree, you tend to think of it as a distinct, clearly defined object, and on a certain level it is. But on a more important level, the tree has no independent existence; rather, it dissolves into a web of relationships. The rain that falls on its leaves, the wind that causes it to sway, the soil that supports it—all form a part of the tree. Ultimately, if you think about it, everything in the universe helps make the tree what it is. It cannot be isolated; its nature changes from moment to moment—it is never the same. This is what we mean when we say that things are 'empty,' that they have no independent existence."

The use of the terms *emptiness* or *nothingness* to define *sunyata* has led many Westerners to think of Buddhism as nihilistic. It is often assumed that its followers are an apathetic lot who do not care if they live or die. Ironically enough, Tashi once expressed similar sentiments in reference to Christianity. "Everything is all laid out for you," he said. "Everything has been determined by God and is controlled by Him. It must make people very apathetic. There seems to be no room in Christianity for personal growth in the way that there is in Buddhism. Through spiritual practice we have an opportunity to develop ourselves."

Buddhism does not say that nothing exists, nor does it in any way encourage pessimism. On the contrary, it teaches that once we have understood the nature of the universe, we will realize a lasting happiness that is unaffected by the transient flow of outer events. Our ignorance—our experience of the world through the senses and through conceptualization—prevents us from seeing beyond the ordinary "everyday" world of appearance, where things exist as separate and permanent things. As long as we persist in seeing things in this "ignorant" way, we are in *samsara,* trapped on the wheel of existence.

We are not being asked to deny the "existence" of the world, but to alter our perception of it. Things do exist insofar as we perceive them with our senses. We do have bodies, we do need air to breathe. It is a question of emphasis. We are not being told to abandon the world as perceived by our senses, but rather to see it in a different light. The Buddha taught that beyond this world created by our own senses and limitations, the phenomenal world dissolves into a dynamic process. The true nature of reality lies beyond the realm of language and linear analysis.

Tashi would often quote from the renowned scholar Nagarjuna: "Those who believe in existence are stupid like cattle, but those who believe in nonexistence are still more stupid. [Things are] not existent, not nonexistent, not both and not something that is not both."

It is said that the universe is like an endless river. Its totality, the unity, does not change, yet at the same time it is in constant motion. The river as a whole exists, but you cannot say what it consists of; you cannot stop the flow and examine it. Everything is in movement and inextricably intertwined.

Tashi again: "Everything is subject to the law of dependent origination. As Nagarjuna said, 'Origin through relations is the Buddha's rich profound treasure.' On this level our categories, distinctions, and labels—'you' and 'I,' 'mind' and 'matter'—become one and disappear. What we take to be solid and substantial is in fact changing from moment to moment. Just in the same way that the tree is 'empty,' the 'self' is empty. If you reflect on it, you too dissolve as part of everything else around you. The 'self,' or ego, is ultimately no more separate than anything else in the universe."

The delusion that the self exists independently is perhaps the greatest obstacle on the path to enlightenment. The belief in absolute, permanent existence leads to a cycle of endless craving, and the craving brings suffering. In our attachment to the notion of a separate self and separate things, we end up constantly striving and reaching for something new. Yet as soon as we have attained what we are seeking, the luster is gone and we set our sights elsewhere. Satisfaction is rare and brief; we are forever frustrated.

> There is no other way to please the Buddha
> Than to please all sentient beings.

Tashi would often remind me that knowledge and understanding were not sufficient in themselves. In fact they could be dangerous, he would say, if not accompanied by compassion. "The Dalai Lama has said that his true religion is kindness. Look at our prayers, they always emphasize concern for others":

> By the force of the noble, virtuous works done in this way,
> My parents who have brought me up kindly,
> The teachers from whom I got my Bodhicitta initiation,
> All the diamond brothers, with cordial relationship,
> All those persons with whom I have material and property relationship,
> May they attain the state of Buddhahood very soon.

In Buddhist teachings, compassion constitutes the so-called method of enlightenment. The poet-sage Milarepa said: "The notion of emptiness engenders compassion." When the boundaries of indi-

vidual existence have been worn away, you and I, instead of being absolutely separate beings, are aspects of the same unity.

Religion permeates all aspects of life in Ladakh, inseparable from art
and music, culture and agriculture. People are deeply religious. Yet,
from a Western point of view, they appear strangely casual about it.
This apparent paradox struck me particularly strongly in 1976 when
His Holiness the Dalai Lama came for a visit—the first one in many
years. For months before, the sense of anticipation grew. People
painted their houses, printed prayer flags, and stitched new clothes;
they even dismantled their elaborate headdresses, washing the turquoises and corals and refurbishing the felt backing with bright red
cloth. It was to be the Great Wheel, or Kalachakra, Initiation, performed on the banks of the Indus outside Leh. Long before the event,
villagers from all over Ladakh started streaming in, some coming by
bus or truck, thousands more walking or riding for days to reach the
capital.

By the middle of the week-long teaching, the numbers had
swelled to forty thousand. The air was charged with intense devotion,
and yet amazingly at the same time there was almost a carnival atmosphere. One minute the man in front of me was lost in reverence,
his gaze locked on the Dalai Lama; the next minute he would be
laughing at a neighbor's joke; and a while later he seemed to be some-
where else, spinning his prayer wheel almost absentmindedly. During
this religious teaching—for many of those present, the most important event of their lifetime—people came and went, laughing and
gossiping. There were picnics and everywhere children—playing,
running, calling out to each other.

Attending the ceremonies was a young Frenchman who had studied Buddhism in Dharamsala, the Dalai Lama's residence in exile. He
took his new religion very seriously and was shocked by the Ladakhis. "These people are not serious. I thought they were supposed
to be Buddhists," he said scornfully. Even though I knew there was
something wrong about his reaction, I was not sure how to respond.
I too had grown up in a culture in which religion was separated from

A festival at Phyang Monastery. The large thanka *is unrolled only once a year.*

the rest of life. It was something a small minority did on Sunday mornings, solemnly and seriously, but that was all.

From daily prayers to annual festivals, the entire calendar is shaped by religious beliefs and practices. The day of the full moon, which always falls on the fifteenth of the Tibetan lunar month, is when the Buddha was conceived, attained enlightenment, and died. Every other week of the month also has its religious significance. The tenth day, for instance, marks the birthday of Guru Rinpoche, who brought Buddhism to Tibet from India. On this day villagers gather in one another's houses to eat and drink while reading religious texts. For *nyeness,* in the first month of the Tibetan calendar, people assemble to fast and meditate together in the *gonpa,* or monastery. On holy days, the family often prints new prayer flags. Cloth in the five holy colors—red, blue, green, yellow, and white—is pressed onto inked carved wooden blocks. The new flags are placed on top of the old, which are never removed, but left to slowly disintegrate, spreading their message on the winds.

Every house is filled with reminders of the region's Buddhist heritage. The kitchen stove is decorated with a *spallbi,* an elaborate knot with no beginning and no end—the knot of prosperity. It is one of the eight lucky symbols of Tibetan Buddhism, which are often depicted in frescoes in the guest room. In addition to the prayer flags strung from corner to corner on every rooftop, there is often a large flagpole in front of the house. This *tarchen* signifies that the house chapel contains all sixteen volumes of the basic Mahayana texts, the *Prajnaparamita,* or books of "perfect wisdom." On one of the exterior walls, you may also see a little balcony with three *chortens (rigs-sum-gompo)*—one orange, one blue, and one white—symbolizing wisdom, strength, and compassion.

Other symbols from earlier times have also been incorporated into present-day Buddhism. On the roof is a *lhato,* a little chimney of mud topped with a bunch of willow branches and a wooden arrow. This is for the protective deity of the house. It contains a vessel filled with grains, water, and precious metals that are changed every New Year to assure continued prosperity. One of the outside walls may have a *sazgo namgo* (literally, "earth door, sky door"). The skull of a sheep or dog is attached to a diamond-shaped web of wood and wool inset with the names and pictures of the owner and his wife. An inscription on it reads, "May these doors—of the earth and of the sky—be protected from evil spirits." Sometimes the house will be decorated with red markings—little figures, rows of dots, and swastikas—to please the *tsan,* a spirit that rides a white horse. From the front, this spirit looks beautiful; but his back, which he exposes if angered, is hideously raw, and to see it can cause grave misfortune.

The Ladakhis have a relaxed attitude to their spirits. Ceremonies are performed to appease them, but people certainly do not live in fear of them. In fact, they do not seem absolutely sure of their existence. "Do you think the spirits are real?" I once asked Sonam. "Well, they say they exist," he answered slowly. "I've never seen any, but who knows."

The role of the monasteries in Tibetan culture has often led people to describe the society as feudal. Initially, I too assumed that the relationship between the monasteries and the rest of the population was an exploitative one. Some monasteries own a lot of land, which is worked by the village as a whole. There are also farmers who, in addition to their own land, cultivate monastery fields in return for some of the yield.

On a broader societal level, however, the monasteries offer real economic benefit. In fact they provide "social security" for the entire community, ensuring that no one goes hungry. If an individual family should find itself with too many mouths to feed, any number of sons—usually the younger ones—become monks. In the monastery they are provided for by the community in exchange for religious services. The process of give and take between the monastery and village sustains a rich cultural and religious tradition in which all members of society are involved and benefits accrue to everyone. Moreover, anyone, male or female, young or old, can opt for celibacy and spiritual devotion as an alternative to the life of a married householder.

As a monk, Angchuk's younger brother Rinchen is respected, though he does not hold the same position as some of the more learned monks or reincarnate lamas, who are venerated for their spe-

*Phuktal Monastery, in Zanskar. In addition to their spiritual
role, monasteries help to provide economic security.*

cial powers and knowledge. Rinchen has a great deal of freedom, despite certain well-defined duties. Though he has his own rooms at the
monastery, he spends much of his time performing religious ceremonies in individual houses, not only in Tongde itself, but in the
neighboring villages of Shadi and Kumik. Throughout the year, especially at the time of sowing and harvest, important rituals are performed in the chapel of every house. These keep him very busy and
are also his main means of support. Each family pays him for his services, increasingly these days in cash. He still has his room at home,
where he sleeps from time to time. When he is there, he does his
share of household chores; his special skill is sewing.

On a number of occasions throughout the year, the monasteries
are home to important ceremonies and festivals involving several
days, even weeks, of ritual and prayer. During Yarnas, which takes
place in summer, the monks stay indoors for up to a month, to avoid
unwillingly treading on and killing insects. One of the biggest events
of the year is the Cham dance, during which the basic teachings of
Vadjrayana Buddhism are enacted in theatrical form and an effigy of

the enemy of all people—the ego—is ceremoniously killed. Hundreds, sometimes thousands, of villagers from all around come to watch the monks dancing in splendidly colorful masks, representing various figures of the Tibetan pantheon, all of which have a deeper symbolic meaning. The sounds of horns and drums blend with the chanting of mantras and laughter.

"As long as there is ignorance, there is a need for ritual," the head lama of Stakna Monastery once told me. "It is a ladder that may be discarded once we have attained a certain level of spiritual development." The rich fabric of ceremony and ritual in Ladakh, though an important part of religious practice, is not as central to the Buddhist teachings as it might appear. For me, the most profound expression of Buddhism in Ladakh lies in the more subtle values and attitudes of the people, from the simplest farmer to the most educated monk.

The Ladakhi attitude to life—and death—seems to be based on an intuitive understanding of impermanence and a consequent lack of attachment. Again and again I have been struck by this attitude in my Ladakhi friends. Rather than clinging to an idea of how things should be, they seem blessed with the ability to actively welcome things as they are. For instance, during the middle of the harvest it can snow or rain, ruining the barley and wheat that have been cultivated with such care for many months. And yet people remain completely unperturbed, often joking about their predicament.

Even death is more readily accepted. In my second year in Ladakh, a good friend of mine lost her two-month-old baby. I thought she would be distraught, and when I first saw her, she was clearly upset. But there was a difference. Although, as she told me, she was extremely saddened, her belief in reincarnation meant that death did not have the same sense of finality as it does for us.

The Ladakhi conception of reality is circular, one of a constant returning. There is not the sense that this life is the only opportunity. Death is as much a beginning as an end, a passing from one birth to the next, not a final dissolution.

Ladakhi attitudes seem to be influenced by meditation. Although deep meditation is rarely practiced outside the monastic community, people spend significant periods of time in what you might call a semi-meditative state. Older people in particular recite mantras as they walk and as they work. Often a conversation will be punctuated with snatches of prayer: a few words and then, in the same breath, the hallowed refrain *"Om mani padme hum, om mani padme hum."* Recent research in the West suggests that during meditation, the mode of consciousness that perceives in wholes or patterns is dominant. This would play a role in shaping the Ladakhis' holistic or contextual world view—a world view that is characteristic even of those who have little knowledge of Buddhist teachings.

It could be argued that even the Ladakhi language exhibits traces of Buddhism. Compared with any Western language that I know, Ladakhi seems to put a greater emphasis on relativity. The language obliges one to express more of the context of what one is trying to say. Most strikingly, the verb *to be* has more than twenty variations, depending on the specifics of the situation—in particular, on the relative intimacy of both the speaker and the listener with the subject matter. Unlike Westerners, Ladakhis never express themselves with certitude about something they have not experienced. Any event in which they have not personally participated will be described using verbs that reflect the limitations of their knowledge: "It is said that . . . ," "It appears that . . . ," "It is probable that. . . " If I ask someone, "Is it a big house?" he or she will be likely to answer, "It seemed big to me."

Even when people have personal experience, they are far more reluctant than we are to categorize and judge. Good and bad, fast and slow, here and there; these are not sharply different qualities. In the same way, Ladakhis will not think in terms of a fundamental opposition, for instance, between mind and body or reason and intuition. Ladakhis experience the world through what they call their *semba*, best translated as a cross between "heart" and "mind." This reflects the Buddhist insistence that Wisdom and Compassion are inseparable.

CHAPTER SEVEN

JOIE DE VIVRE

You mean, everyone isn't as happy as we are?
Tsering Dolma

At the end of one summer, I went with Ngawang Paljor, a sixty-year-old *thanka* painter, to Srinagar in Kashmir. He was traditionally dressed in woolen *goncha,* hat, and yak-hair boots, and in the Kashmiris' eyes he was obviously from the "backward" region of Ladakh. Wherever we went, people made fun of him; he was constantly teased and taunted. Every taxi driver, shopkeeper, and passerby in some way managed to poke fun at him. "Look at that stupid hat!" "Look at those silly boots!" "You know, those primitive people never wash!" It seemed incomprehensible to me, but Ngawang remained completely unaffected by it all. He was enjoying the visit and never lost the twinkle in his eye. Though he was perfectly aware of what was going on, it just didn't seem to matter to him. He was smiling and polite, and when people jeeringly shouted the traditional Ladakhi greeting, *"Jule, jule!"* he simply answered *"Jule, jule!"* back. "Why don't you get angry?" I asked. *"Chi choen?"* ("What's the point?") was his reply.

Ngawang's equanimity was not unusual. The Ladakhis possess an irrepressible joie de vivre. Their sense of joy seems so firmly anchored within them that circumstances cannot shake it loose. You

83

cannot spend any time at all in Ladakh without being won over by the contagious laughter.

At first I couldn't believe that the Ladakhis could be as happy as they appeared. It took me a long time to accept that the smiles I saw were real. Then, in my second year there, while at a wedding, I sat back and observed the guests enjoying themselves. Suddenly I heard myself saying, "Aha, they really are that happy." Only then did I recognize that I had been walking around with cultural blinders on, convinced that the Ladakhis could not be as happy as they seemed. Hidden behind the jokes and laughter had to be the same frustration, jealousy, and inadequacy as in my own society. In fact, without knowing it, I had been assuming that there were no significant cultural differences in the human potential for happiness. It was a surprise for me to realize that I had been making such unconscious assumptions, and as a result I think I became more open to experiencing what was really there.

Of course the Ladakhis have sorrows and problems, and of course they feel sad when faced with illness or death. What I have seen is not an absolute difference; it is a question of degree. Yet the difference in degree is all-significant. As I return each year to the industrialized world, the contrast becomes more and more obvious. With so much of our lives colored by a sense of insecurity or fear, we have difficulty in letting go and feeling at one with ourselves and our surroundings. The Ladakhis, on the other hand, seem to possess an extended, inclusive sense of self. They do not, as we do, retreat behind boundaries of fear and self-protection; in fact, they seem to be totally lacking in what we would call pride. This doesn't mean a lack of self-respect. On the contrary, their self-respect is so deep-rooted as to be unquestioned.

I was with about fifteen Ladakhis and two students from Calcutta on the back of a truck taking us along the bumpy and dusty road from Zanskar. As the journey went on, the students became restless and uncomfortable and began pushing at a middle-aged Ladakhi who had made a seat for himself out of a sack of vegetables. Before long, the older man stood up so that the students—who were about twenty years younger than him—could sit down. When, after about two hours, we stopped for a rest, the students indicated to the Ladakhi that they wanted him to fetch water for them; he fetched the water. They then more or less ordered him to make a fire and boil tea for them.

He was effectively being treated as a servant—almost certainly for the first time in his life. Yet there was nothing remotely servile in his behavior; he merely did what was asked of him as he might for a friend—without obsequiousness and with no loss of dignity. I was fuming, but he and the other Ladakhis, far from being angered or embarrassed by the way he was being treated, found it all amusing and nothing more. The old man was so relaxed about who he was that he had no need to prove himself.

I have never met people who seem so healthy emotionally, so secure, as the Ladakhis. The reasons are, of course, complex and spring from a whole way of life and world view. But I am sure that the most important factor is the sense that you are a part of something much larger than yourself, that you are inextricably connected to others and to your surroundings.

The Ladakhis belong to their place on earth. They are bonded to that place through intimate daily contact, through a knowledge about their immediate environment with its changing seasons, needs, and limitations. They are aware of the living context in which they find themselves. The movement of the stars, the sun, and moon are familiar rhythms that influence their daily activities.

Just as importantly, the Ladakhis' larger sense of self has something to do with the close ties between people. At that wedding, I watched the *paspun* group as they laughed and joked together and then sat quietly drinking tea, lost in their own thoughts for long periods without the need to exchange a word. They had shared many experiences—grieving and rejoicing. And they had worked together, supporting one another, during the ceremonies that mark the important transitions of life. I suddenly gained an insight into the depth of their relationships.

In traditional Ladakhi society, everyone, including aunts and uncles, monks and nuns, belongs to a highly interdependent commu-

*The Ladakhis' remarkable contentedness is the product of close
and intimate connections to other people and the land.*

nity. A mother is never left on her own, separated from all her
children. She always remains a part of their lives and those of their
children.

Before feeling my way into Ladakhi culture, I had thought that
leaving home was part of growing up, a necessary step toward becoming an adult. I now believe that large extended families and small
intimate communities form a better foundation for the creation of
mature, balanced individuals. A healthy society is one that encourages close social ties and mutual interdependence, granting each individual a net of unconditional emotional support. Within this
nurturing framework, individuals feel secure enough to become
quite free and independent. Paradoxically, I have found the Ladakhis
less emotionally dependent than we are in industrial society. There is
love and friendship, but it is not intense or grasping—not a possession of one person by another. I once saw a mother greeting her
eighteen-year-old son when he returned home after being away for a
year. She seemed surprisingly calm, as though she had not missed
him. It took me a long time to understand this behavior. I thought my

Ladakhi friends reacted strangely when I arrived back after being away for the winter. I had brought presents I knew they would like. I expected them to be pleased to see me and happy at the gifts. But to them it was as if I had not been gone. They thanked me for the presents, but not in the way that I was hoping. I was wanting them to look excited and confirm our special friendship. I was disappointed. Whether I had been away for six months or a day, they treated me in the same way.

I came to realize, however, that the ability to adjust to any situation, to feel happy regardless of the circumstances, was a tremendous strength. I came to appreciate the easy, relaxed attitude of my Ladakhi friends and to like being treated as though I had never been away. Ladakhis do not seem to be as attached to anything as we are. Most of them are, of course, not completely without the attachments that so affect our lives. But again, there is a difference—an all-pervasive difference—in degree. One may be unhappy to see a friend leave or to lose something valuable, but not *that* unhappy.

If I ask a Ladakhi, "Do you enjoy going to Leh, or do you prefer staying in the village?" I am likely to get the answer "I am happy if I go to Leh; and if I don't go, I am also happy." It really does not matter so much one way or the other. The Ladakhis enjoy a feast more than everyday food, and they would rather be comfortable than uncomfortable, healthy rather than ill. But, finally, their contentedness and peace of mind do not seem dependent on such outside circumstances; these qualities come more from within. The Ladakhis' relationships to others and to their surroundings have helped nurture a sense of inner calm and contentedness, and their religion has reminded them that you can be healthy, warm, comfortable, and well fed, yet so long as you remain "ignorant," you will not be happy.

Contentment comes from feeling and understanding yourself to be part of the flow of life, relaxing and moving with it. If it starts to pour with rain just as you set out on a long journey, why be miserable? Maybe you would not have preferred it, but the Ladakhis' attitude is "Why be unhappy?"

PART TWO

CHANGE

CHAPTER EIGHT

THE COMING OF THE WEST

Riding on their imperial horses,
Flying like kings,
Thinking that they've understood everything.
Do they not realize that even birds fly?

Tashi Rabgyas, angered by tourists, 1980

I lived through most of the experiences described in the preceding pages at a time when Ladakh had not yet been affected by the Western world in any significant way. When I first arrived in 1975, life in the villages was still based on the same foundations as it had been for centuries, evolving in its own environment, according to its own principles. The region had been protected from both colonialism and development by its lack of resources, its inhospitable climate, and its inaccessibility.

Of course the culture had experienced change, from year to year, from generation to generation. Ladakh lay on one of Asia's major trade routes, and had been exposed to the influence of other cultures. But in the old days change had come slowly, allowing for an adaptation from within. Outside influences had been incorporated gradually, on the culture's own terms.

In recent years, however, external forces have descended on the Ladakhis like an avalanche, causing massive and rapid disruption. The Indian army, which had been in Ladakh since 1962 to protect the region from Pakistani and Chinese incursions, had already had an effect on the culture. But the process of change began in earnest in 1974, when the Indian government threw the area open to tourism—a move that was probably intended to place Ladakh firmly on the map as Indian territory. At about the same time, concerted efforts were initiated to develop the district. Until now, development has been concentrated primarily in Leh and its immediate surroundings; roughly 70 percent of the population still lives more or less traditionally. But the psychological impact of modernization has been felt throughout the entire region.

Development policies for Ladakh are formulated in the state government of Kashmir and the central government in Delhi. Ladakh sends one M.P. to Delhi and one representative to the state government. In Ladakh itself, government programs are administered by officials who generally are not Ladakhi and do not speak the language. The head of the administration, or Development Commissioner, is an officer in the Indian administrative service and spends an average of just two to three years in his job. During my sixteen years in Ladakh, there have been no fewer than seven D.C.s.

As everywhere else in the world, development in Ladakh means Western-style development. This process has consisted primarily of building up the so-called "infrastructure"—especially roads and the production of energy. Power represents the largest expense in the government's budget, as evidenced by the twenty years and many millions of dollars spent on the recently completed four-megawatt hydroelectric installation on the Indus River. Western-style medicine and education form the other basic cornerstones. Health centers and schools have now been established in even quite remote villages. Other fundamental changes include a large and growing police force, a court in Leh, banks, and radio and television (the latter still only in Leh and its surroundings).

Spurred on by development efforts, the formal sector has been growing rapidly. The money economy is stimulated at every level, and the government subsidizes an increasing number of imports. From 1985 to 1986, 6,000 tons of wheat and rice were brought into Leh district alone, while 900,000 pounds of hard coke and 50,000 cubic feet of firewood are imported annually. Most of this is subsidized. Traffic is increasing exponentially as many hundreds of trucks a day make the long journey from the Indian plains laden with goods. Jeeps and buses, crammed with thousands of tourists, add to the congestion and air pollution along the road and in the capital.

As a consequence of contact with the modern world, population has been rising at a rate higher than the Indian average in recent years. There was a 31 percent increase from 51,891 in 1971 to 67,733 in 1981. This compares with a rise of only 3 percent from 1901 (32,614) to 1911 (33,434). Coupled with rural migration, this has led to a house-building boom in and around Leh, where the urban sprawl is beginning to resemble the slums that so characterize cities throughout the Third World.

Tourism, with its promise of foreign exchange, is an integral part of the development package. Starting with a handful of visitors in the autumn of 1974, the number had risen to almost 15,000 a year in 1984. The vast majority of these people visit the region in the four-month period from June to September, and almost without exception, they come to Leh, which has a population of roughly 10,000. Tourism has given rise to a boom in related businesses, including the construction of more than a hundred hotels and guesthouses in Leh, where previously there were none.

The impact of tourism on the material culture has been wide-ranging and disturbing. Still more significant, however, has been its impact on people's minds.

CHAPTER NINE

PEOPLE FROM MARS

At one village I witnessed a trekking group armed with cameras,
bon bons, and pens, virtually attack the villagers. Dressed in
fluorescent greens, reds, and blues, they poked their cameras in
unsuspecting faces without a word and then moved on to their
next victim.

Angry tourist, 1990

Imagine living your day-to-day life as usual and suddenly waking up
to find your town invaded by people from another planet. Speaking a
strange tongue and looking even stranger, these extraterrestrials lead
quite extraordinary lives. They do not appear to know what work is,
but enjoy constant leisure. Moreover, they have special powers and
inexhaustible wealth.

Imagine further how your children might react to this experience,
how fascinated they would be. Just think how difficult it would be to
stop them from following these creatures, to convince them that they
were better off staying home with you. How could you prevent
impressionable teenagers, in their search for identity, from being
swept off their feet?

I was in Ladakh from the time tourism started, and was able to observe the process of change from the beginning. Since I spoke the
language fluently, I gained an insight into the intense psychological
pressures that modernization brings. Looking at the modern world
from something of a Ladakhi perspective, I also became aware that

94

our culture looks infinitely more successful from the outside than we experience it on the inside.

With no warning, people from another world descended on Ladakh. Each day many would spend as much as a hundred dollars, an amount roughly equivalent to someone spending fifty thousand dollars a day in America. In the traditional subsistence economy, money played a minor role, used primarily for luxuries—jewelry, silver, and gold. Basic needs—food, clothing, and shelter—were provided for without money. The labor one needed was free of charge, part of an intricate web of human relationships.

In one day a tourist would spend the same amount that a Ladakhi family might in a year. Ladakhis did not realize that money played a completely different role for the foreigners; that back home they needed it to survive; that food, clothing, and shelter all cost money— a lot of money. Compared to these strangers, they suddenly felt poor. During my first years in Ladakh, young children I had never seen before used to run up to me and press apricots into my hands. Now little figures, looking shabbily Dickensian in threadbare Western clothing, greet foreigners with an empty outstretched hand. They demand "one pen, one pen," a phrase that has become the new mantra of Ladakhi children.

The tourists, for their part, think Ladakhis are backward. The few who experience the hospitality of a village home invariably speak of this as the highlight of their holiday. But most of them can only see Ladakhi culture from the outside, and they view it out of the experience of their own culture and economy. They assume that money plays the same role in Ladakh as at home. If they meet a Ladakhi who is earning only two dollars a day, they are horrified and show it. Implicitly or explicitly, they say to him, "Oh, you poor thing. I'd better give you a big tip." To Western eyes, Ladakhis look poor. Tourists can only see the material side of the culture—worn-out woolen robes, the *dzo* pulling a plough, the barren land. They cannot see peace of mind or the quality of family and community relations. They cannot see the psychological, social, and spiritual wealth of the Ladakhis.

Besides giving the illusion that all Westerners are multimillionaires, the tourist also helps perpetuate another faulty image of modern life—that we never work. It looks as though our technologies do the work for us. In industrial society today, we actually spend more hours working than people in rural, agrarian economies. But that is not how it looks to the Ladakhis. For them, work is physical work, walking, and carrying things. A person sitting behind the wheel of a car or pushing buttons on a typewriter doesn't appear to be working.

One day I had spent ten hours writing letters. I was exhausted, stressed, and had a headache. In the evening, when I complained about being tired because of having worked so hard, the family I was living with laughed; they thought I was joking. In their eyes, I had not been working; I had been sitting in front of a table, nice and clean, no sweat on my brow, pushing a pen across a piece of paper. This was not work. Ladakhis have not yet experienced the sort of stress, boredom, or frustration that is so much a part of our lives in the West. Once, I tried to explain the concept of stress to some villagers. "You mean you get angry because you have to work?" was the response.

Every day I saw people from two cultures, a world apart, looking at each other and seeing superficial, one-dimensional images. Tourists see people carrying loads on their backs and walking long distances over high mountain passes and say, "How terrible; what a life of drudgery." They forget that they have traveled thousands of miles and spent thousands of dollars for the pleasure of walking through the same mountains with heavy backpacks. They also forget how much their bodies suffer from lack of use at home. During working hours they get no exercise, so they spend their free time trying to make up for it. Some will even drive to a health club—across a polluted city in rush hour—to sit in a basement, pedaling a bicycle that does not go anywhere. And they actually pay for the privilege.

Development has brought not only tourism, but also Western and Indian films and, more recently, television. Together they provide overwhelming images of luxury and power. There are countless tools and magical gadgets. And there are machines—machines to take pictures, machines to tell the time, machines to make fire, to travel from one place to another, to talk with someone far away. Machines can do

Cultures in collision. Westernized Indian films have had a profound impact on young Ladakhis, making them feel ashamed of their own traditions and values.

everything for you; it is no wonder the tourists look so clean and have such soft, white hands.

In films, the rich, the beautiful, and the brave lead lives filled with excitement and glamor. For the young Ladakhis, the picture they present is irresistible. By contrast, their own lives seem primitive, silly, and inefficient. The one-dimensional view of modern life becomes a slap in the face. They feel stupid and ashamed. They are asked by their parents to choose a way of life that involves working in the fields and getting their hands dirty for very little or no money. Their own culture seems absurd compared with the world of the tourists and film heroes.

For millions of youths in rural areas of the world, modern Western culture appears far superior to their own. It is not surprising since, looking as they do from the outside, all they can see is the material side of the modern world—the side in which Western culture excels. They cannot so readily see the social or psychological dimensions—the stress, the loneliness, the fear of growing old. Nor can they see environmental decay, inflation, or unemployment. On the other hand, they know their own culture inside out, including all its limitations and imperfections.

The sudden influx of Western influence has caused some Ladakhis—the young men in particular—to develop feelings of inferiority. They reject their own culture wholesale, and at the same time eagerly embrace the new one. They rush after the symbols of modernity: sunglasses, Walkmans, and blue jeans several sizes too small—not because they find those jeans more attractive or comfortable, but because they are symbols of modern life.

Modern symbols have also contributed to an increase in aggression in Ladakh. Now young boys see violence glamorized on the screen. From Western-style films, they can easily get the impression that if they want to be modern, they should smoke one cigarette after another, get a fast car, and race through the countryside shooting people left and right!

It has been painful to see the changes in young Ladakhi friends. Of course they do not all turn violent, but they do become angry and less secure. I have seen a gentle culture change—a culture in which men, even young men, were happy to cuddle a baby or to be loving and soft with their grandmothers.

Dawa was about fifteen when I met him, and he was still living in his village. When the tourists started coming, he became a guide. He used his donkeys and mules for trekking, as pack animals. I lost contact with him for several years, but I heard that he had started his own tourist agency—one of the first Ladakhis to do so. Then one day in the bazaar I bumped into a young man wearing the latest fashion gear: metallic sunglasses, a T-shirt advertising an American rock band, skin-tight blue jeans, and basketball shoes. It was Dawa.

"I hardly recognized you," I said in Ladakhi.

"Changed a bit, eh?" he replied proudly in English.

We went to a restaurant crowded with tourists from every part of the globe. Dawa insisted on talking in English.

"You know I'm working for myself now? Business is great, Helena. I have lots of customers and I'm making a lot of money. I have a room in Leh now."

In Ladakh, boys and girls alike are encouraged to develop their nurturing instincts.

"I'm surprised I haven't seen more of you," I said.

"Well, I'm hardly ever here—I collect the groups myself in Srinagar, and spend most of the time trekking and visiting monasteries."

"You like your new life?"

"I like it. Most of the tourists are real VIPs! Not like these Ladakhis who just laze around all day." He grinned at me. "A surgeon from New York gave me this," he said, pointing to his brand-new backpack.

"Do you go back to the village much?"

"Every few months—to take them rice and sugar. And they always want me back to help with the harvest."

"How does it feel to go home?"

"Boring. It's so backward there! We still don't have electricity, and Abi [grandmother] doesn't even want it."

"Maybe she likes the old ways."

"Well, they can be stuck in the old ways if they want, but Ladakh will change around them. We've worked in the fields long enough, Helena; we don't want to work so hard anymore."

"I thought you said Ladakhis just laze around all day."

"I mean they don't know how to get ahead."

Dawa ostentatiously pulled a pack of Marlboros from his pocket. When I turned down his offer, he lit one for himself and leaned toward me with a worried look.

"I had a fight with my girlfriend this morning. I was looking for her when I met you."

"Oh! Who's your girlfriend?"

"I'm not sure I still have a girlfriend, but she's from Holland. She was in one of my tour groups and stayed on to be with me. But she doesn't like it here anymore—she wants to go home. And she wants me to go with her, to live in Holland."

"Would you do that?" I asked.

"I can't leave my family. They need the money I earn. But she can't understand that."

CHAPTER TEN

MONEY MAKES
THE WORLD GO ROUND

We don't have any poverty here.
Tsewang Paljor, 1975

If you could only help us Ladakhis, we're so poor.
Tsewang Paljor, 1983

In the traditional culture, villagers provided for their basic needs without money. They had developed skills that enabled them to grow barley at 12,000 feet and to manage yaks and other animals at even higher elevations. People knew how to build houses with their own hands from the materials of the immediate surroundings. The only thing they actually needed from outside the region was salt, for which they traded. They used money in only a limited way, mainly for luxuries.

Now, suddenly, as part of the international money economy, Ladakhis find themselves ever more dependent—even for vital needs—on a system that is controlled by faraway forces. They are vulnerable to decisions made by people who do not even know that Ladakh exists. If the value of the dollar changes, it will ultimately have an effect on the Indian rupee. This means that Ladakhis who need money to survive are now under the control of the managers of international finance. Living off the land, they had been their own masters.

At first, people were not aware of the fact that the new economy creates dependence; money appeared to be only an advantage. Since it traditionally had been a good thing, bringing luxuries from far away, more of it seemed to be an unconditional improvement. Now you can buy all sorts of exotic things that you could not before, like three-minute noodles and digital watches.

As people find themselves dependent on a very different economic system for all their needs and vulnerable to the vagaries of inflation, it is not strange that they should become preoccupied with money. For two thousand years in Ladakh, a kilo of barley has been a kilo of barley, but now you cannot be sure of its value. If you have ten rupees today, it can buy two kilos of barley, but how do you know how much it will buy tomorrow? "It's terrible," Ladakhi friends would say to me, "everyone is getting so greedy. Money was never important before, but now it's all people can think about."

Traditionally, people were conscious of the limits of resources and of their personal responsibilities. I have heard older people say: "What on earth is going to happen if we start dividing the land and increasing in numbers? It can never work." But the new economy cuts people off from the earth. Paid work is in the city, where you cannot see the water and soil on which your life depends. In the village you can see with the naked eye how many mouths the land can support. A given area can only produce so much, so you know that it is important to keep the population stable. Not so in the city; there it is just a question of how much money you have, and the birth rate is no longer significant. More money will buy more food. And it can grow much faster than wheat or barley, which are dependent on nature with her own laws, rhythms, and limits. Money does not seem to have any limits; an advertisement for the local Jammu-Kashmir Bank says, "Your money grows quickly with us."

For centuries, people worked as equals and friends—helping one another by turn. Now that there is paid labor during the harvest, the person paying the money wants to pay as little as possible, while the person receiving wants to have as much as possible. Relationships change. The money becomes a wedge between people, pushing them further and further apart.

*Traditionally, all agricultural work is shared—both within the family
and through reciprocal arrangements between households.*

The house had a festive atmosphere whenever Tsering and Sonam
Dolma's friends came to work with them as part of the traditional
lhangsde practice. Sonam used to cook special food for the occasion.
But in the last couple of years, the practice has gradually disappeared
and their farm near Leh is increasingly dependent on paid labor.
Sonam complains bitterly about rising prices and resents having to
pay high wages. The festive atmosphere of friends working together
has gone; these laborers are strangers, sometimes Nepalis or Indians
from the plains who have no common language.

The changing economy makes it difficult to remain a farmer. Previously, with cooperative labor between people, farmers had no need
for money. Now, unable to pay larger and larger wages for farm hands,
some are forced to abandon the villages to earn money in the city. For
those who stay, the pressure increases to grow food for profit, instead
of food for themselves. Cash cropping becomes the norm as farmers
are pushed by the forces of development to become dependent on
the market economy.

The new economy also increases the gap between rich and poor.

In the traditional economy there were differences in wealth, but its accumulation had natural limits. You could only care for so many yaks or store so many kilos of barley. Money, on the other hand, is easily stored in the bank, and the rich get richer and the poor get poorer.

I knew a man named Lobzang who had an antique shop in Leh. Like many Ladakhi shopkeepers, he had given up farming and come to Leh to make money, but his wife and children still lived in the village. He wanted the best for his children, and as soon as he could afford the housing, he planned to bring them to town to get the benefits of an education and, in particular, to learn English.

I had just dropped into his shop to say hello when an old man from Lobzang's village came in to sell his butter jars. It was a full day's journey on foot and by bus from the village. The old man probably planned to spend a couple of days with relatives in Leh, buying supplies to take back to the village with the money from the butter jars. He looked dignified in his traditional burgundy woolen robes. He put two jars on the counter. They had the warm patina that comes from generations of constant handling. They were made of fine-grained apricot wood and had a simple elegance that would certainly appeal to tourists. "They're lovely," I said. "What will you keep your butter in without them?" "We keep it in used milk tins," he said.

They argued about the price. Apparently a few weeks earlier, Lobzang had promised him a much higher price than he was willing to offer now. He pointed to some cracks in the jars and refused to raise his offer. I knew he would get ten times as much when he sold the jars to the tourists. The old man threw me an imploring look, but what could I say? He left the shop with a disappointed stoop to his shoulders and enough money to buy a few kilos of sugar.

"You shouldn't have said they were lovely." Lobzang scolded me. "I had to give him more."

"But he's from your own village. Do you have to bargain so hard with him?"

"I hate it, but I have to. Besides, a stranger would have given him even less."

CHAPTER ELEVEN

FROM LAMA TO ENGINEER

Who needs monks?
Ladakhi youth, 1984

In watching Ladakh get "developed," it has been difficult to say which is the more fundamental agent of change, money or technology. But it is obvious that they are closely interlinked and form the cornerstones of a systemic transformation of society.

Ladakh has not yet experienced far-reaching technological change, but this will certainly come if present trends continue. And the changes that have already occurred are enough to demonstrate some of the "side effects" of Western-style technological development. An example is the new diesel-powered mill in Leh. It grinds grain many times faster than the old water wheels, but people have to transport their wheat and barley many miles from the villages and pay for it to be ground. The greater speed has the effect of heating the grain, so that it reduces its nutritional value. Furthermore, the mill spews polluting fumes into the air.

In the village, technology was based on traditional knowledge and used local resources. The plough was made of local wood, and its iron tip was forged by the village blacksmith. The yak or *dzo* that pulled it was fed on the wild grasses of high pastures. Thus almost all the skills and materials needed to plough were renewable and readily available.

It is easy to romanticize traditional technologies, but it is also common in the West to ignore many of their benefits. Tashi Rabgyas would sometimes talk about the advantages of the old over the new, and in particular of working with animals rather than machines: "They become your friends, you relate to them. If they have done a particularly good job, if they have worked particularly hard, you might give them something special to eat. But machines are dead, you have no relationship with them. When you work with machines, you become like them, you become dead yourself."

Of course, ploughing in the traditional way took a long time—it might take half a day to complete an acre. Naturally a farmer who, unlike Tashi, had never been outside Ladakh, would welcome a technology that saves time. Why spend half a day when a tractor can do the same job in half an hour? The truth is, however, that the new faster technologies do not in the end save time.

In the traditional economy, time was plentiful and limited only by the course of the seasons. However much work there was to be done, life was lived at a human pace and everyone could afford to be patient. By contrast, the modern economy turns time into a commodity—something that can be bought and sold—and suddenly it is quantified and divided into the tiniest fragments. Time becomes something costly, and as people acquire new "time-saving" technologies the pace of life only gets faster.

The Ladakhis now have less time for each other and for themselves. As a result, they are losing their once-acute sensitivity to the nuances of the world around them—the ability, for instance, to detect the slightest variations in the weather, or in the movement of the stars. A friend from the Markha Valley summed it up for me: "I can't understand it. My sister in the capital, she now has all these things that do the work faster. She just buys her clothes in a shop, she has a jeep, a telephone, a gas cooker. All of these things save so much time, and yet when I go to visit her, she doesn't have time to talk to me."

One of the most striking lessons that changing Ladakh has taught me is that while the tools and machines of the modern world in themselves save time, the new way of life as a whole has the effect of taking time away. As a result of development, Ladakhis in the modern sector have become part of an economic system in which people have to compete at the speed of the available technologies. This, it seems to me, is a tremendously important point. Once the society in which you operate has telephones, you are at a great disadvantage—economically as well as psychologically—if you do not have one. Delivering your messages in person is in practice not a real alternative. Likewise, once there are cars and buses, you no longer have the choice of walking or riding animals. You cannot wake up in the morning and say, "Now today shall I drive or walk to work?" The pace of your life is determined for you.

I remember the first time I went with Sonam to visit his family in Hemis Shukpachan. As we sat around the kitchen stove, he described the tourists he'd seen in Leh. "They look so busy," he said. "They never seem to sit still. Just click, click, click . . ." He pretended to take a photograph, to the incomprehension of his audience. Then he patted his little sister on the head, imitating a tourist: " 'Here's a ball-point pen for you.' They're always rushing like this," he said, jumping up and running jerkily around the kitchen. "Why are they in such a hurry?"

Technological change also increases the gap between rich and poor. The Ladakhi who goes zooming past in a car leaves the pedestrian behind in the dust, both physically and psychologically. And new social problems arise as people start living in one place and working in another. Women are left on their own and communities are divided.

Lobzang was a government driver. When he retired, he bought a jeep and brought it back with him to his village. In the summer he used it to ferry tourists to the monasteries, and the rest of the year he drove his neighbors to and from Leh, for a fee. As a result, his relationship with the other villagers began to change—he now had something the others did not, and was no longer quite one of them.

"In the future, and it's probably not that far away, we'll be able to construct a machine and you'll be able to push a button and anything you want will come out—from a plastic bucket to an apple." This is what Tsering Dorje told me just after he had returned from university in Kashmir, where he had become very interested in physics. When I expressed surprise, he explained, "Since everything is ulti-

Symbols of the old, symbols of the new.

mately made out of the same atoms, there's no reason why we can't put them together to create whatever we want." Tsering's sentiments reflect a fundamental change in attitudes and values—the birth of a new world view in Ladakh, a world view that gives human beings greatly increased power over the rest of creation. In the traditional society, the most respected person was the lama. In the modern sector, it is the engineer.

While I was staying with the Smanla family in the village of Stok, I heard the father and grandmother talking about the future of the youngest son. Their conversation was typical of many. Abi (Grandmother) wanted the boy to become a monk. She said every family should have someone in the monastery. But the father was eager for him to have a modern education so he could get a job in the government. Even though the father was religious, he wanted his son to learn the new ways. An older son, Nyingma, was already studying at the agricultural college in Kashmir. Abi said, "Look at what happened to Nyingma when he went away to school. Now he has no respect for religion anymore." "Yes," said the father, "but soon he'll be able to earn money, and that's necessary these days. How can we know what's best? Here in the village we don't understand the new ways."

The world views of the lama and the engineer are very different. The old beliefs were based on a description of reality that emphasized the unity or dependent origination of all life, whereas the new scientific perspective emphasizes its separateness. It seems to say that we stand apart—outside the rest of creation. And to gain a greater understanding of the way nature works, we simply have to split matter into smaller and smaller fragments and examine the various pieces in isolation.

The shift from lama to engineer represents a shift from ethical values that encourage an empathetic and compassionate relationship with all that lives toward a value-free "objectivity" that has no ethical foundation.

CHAPTER TWELVE

LEARNING THE WESTERN WAY

Even if you know, it's better to ask another.
Ladakhi saying

No one could deny the value of real education, that is, the widening and enrichment of knowledge. But today education has become something quite different. It isolates children from their culture and from nature, training them instead to become narrow specialists in a Westernized urban environment. This process is particularly striking in Ladakh, where modern schooling acts almost as a blindfold, preventing children from seeing the context in which they live. They leave school unable to use their own resources, unable to function in their own world.

With the exception of religious training in the monasteries, the traditional culture had no separate process called "education." Education was the product of an intimate relationship with the community and its environment. Children learned from grandparents, family, and friends. Helping with the sowing, for instance, they would learn that on one side of the village it was a little warmer, on the other side a little colder. From their own experience children would come to distinguish between different strains of barley and the specific growing conditions each strain preferred. They learned to recognize even the tiniest wild plant and how to use it, and how to pick out a particular animal on a faraway mountain slope. They learned about

connections, process, and change, about the intricate web of fluctuating relationships in the natural world around them.

For generation after generation, Ladakhis grew up learning how to
provide themselves with clothing and shelter; how to make shoes out
of yak skin and robes from the wool of sheep; how to build houses out
of mud and stone. Education was location-specific and nurtured an
intimate relationship with the living world. It gave children an intuitive awareness that allowed them, as they grew older, to use resources in an effective and sustainable way.

None of that knowledge is provided in the modern school. Children are trained to become specialists in a technological, rather than
an ecological, society. School is a place to forget traditional skills and,
worse, to look down on them.

Western education first came to Ladakhi villages in the 1970s. Today there are about two hundred schools. The basic curriculum is a
poor imitation of that taught in other parts of India, which itself is an
imitation of British education. There is almost nothing Ladakhi
about it. Once, while visiting a classroom in Leh, I saw a drawing in a
textbook of a child's bedroom that could have been in London or
New York. It showed a pile of neatly folded handkerchiefs on a four-
poster bed and gave instructions as to which drawer of the vanity unit
to keep them in. Equally absurd and inappropriate were the examples in Sonam's younger sister's schoolbooks. Once, for homework,
she was supposed to figure out the angle of incidence that The Lean-
ing Tower of Pisa makes with the ground. Another time she was
struggling with an English translation of the *Iliad.*

Most of the skills Ladakhi children learn in school will never be of
real use to them. They receive a poor version of an education appropriate for a New Yorker. They learn out of books written by people
who have never set foot in Ladakh, who know nothing about growing
barley at 12,000 feet or about making houses out of sun-dried bricks.

In every corner of the world today, the process called "education"
is based on the same assumptions and the same Eurocentric model.
The focus is on faraway facts and figures, a universal knowledge. The
books propagate information that is meant to be appropriate for the
entire planet. But since only a kind of knowledge that is far removed

from specific ecosystems and cultures can be universally applicable, what children learn is essentially synthetic, divorced from the living context. If they go on to higher education, they may learn about building houses, but these houses will be of concrete and steel, the universal box. So too, if they study agriculture, they will learn about industrial farming: chemical fertilizers and pesticides, large machinery and hybrid seeds. The Western educational system is making us all poorer by teaching people around the world to use the same resources, ignoring those of their own environment. In this way education is creating artificial scarcity and inducing competition.

One of the clearest examples of this process in Ladakh is the way in which the yak and its local hybrids are being replaced by the Jersey cow. The yak is important in the traditional economy. It is an animal perfectly adapted to the local environment, actually preferring to stay high up in the vicinity of the glaciers, at about 16,000 feet or more. It covers vast distances, climbing up and down vertical slopes to graze, thriving on the sparse vegetation that grows in this difficult terrain. Its long hair protects it against the cold, and despite its enormous size, it can balance with remarkable grace on a ragged rock face. The yak provides fuel, meat, and labor, and hair from which blankets are woven. The female also gives a limited amount of very rich milk, an average of three liters a day.

According to the modern way of looking at things, the yak is "inefficient." Agricultural experts who have received a Western education tend to be scornful of it. "The *drimo* [female yak] gives only three liters of milk a day," they say. "What we need is Jersey cows—they give thirty liters a day." The experts' training does not allow them to see the broader cultural, economic, and ecological implications of their recommendations. The yak, as it grazed, was gathering together energy from vast distances—energy that, in addition to fuel, was ultimately being used by people in the form of food, clothing, and labor. The Jersey cow, by contrast, cannot even walk up to 16,000 feet, let alone survive there. She has to stay down at 10,000 or 11,000 feet, where people live, and has to have a special shelter. She has to be stall fed on specially cultivated fodder.

Modern education not only ignores local resources, but, worse

Perfectly suited to their environment, yaks graze at high-altitude pastures.

still, makes Ladakhi children think of themselves and their culture as inferior. They are robbed of their self-esteem. Everything in school promotes the Western model and, as a direct consequence, makes them ashamed of their own traditions.

In 1986, schoolchildren were asked to imagine Ladakh in the year 2000. A little girl wrote "Before 1974, Ladakh was not known to the world. People were uncivilized. There was a smile on every face. They don't need money. Whatever they had was enough for them." In another essay a child wrote "They do sing their own songs like they feel disgrace, but they sing English and Hindi songs with great interest. . . . But in these days we find that maximum people and persons didn't wear our own dress, like feeling disgrace."

Education pulls people away from agriculture into the city, where they become dependent on the money economy. In traditional Ladakh there was no such thing as unemployment. But in the modern sector there is now intense competition for a very limited number of paying jobs, principally in the government. As a result, unemployment is already a serious problem.

Modern education has brought obvious benefits, like improvements in the rate of literacy and numeracy. It has also enabled the Ladakhis to be more informed about the forces at play in the world outside. In so doing, however, it has divided Ladakhis from each other and the land and put them on the lowest rung of the global economic ladder.

CHAPTER THIRTEEN

A PULL TO THE CENTER

There will be nothing left which can prove the culture of Ladakh.
From an essay on change in Ladakh—Dolma, age eight

Not long ago, I was traveling on a bus from Leh to the village of Sakti. As so often happens, a woman asked me about life back in my country. "It sounds wonderful," she said. "Life must be so easy for you." "No, it's not quite like you imagine," I replied. "You'd be surprised—there are many disadvantages too." I told her about our problems—how many people live packed together in big cities and yet do not even know the names of their neighbors; how parents do not have time for their children; how the air is so polluted, the streets so noisy. When I had finished, a man from farther back in the bus called out to the woman, asking her what I had said. "She said life over there is just the way it is in Leh these days!" the woman shouted back.

When I first came to Leh, it was a lovely town. It had only two paved streets, and a motor vehicle was a rare sight. Cows were the most likely cause of congestion. The air was crystal clear, so clear that the snow peaks on the far side of the valley, twenty or so miles away, seemed close enough to touch. Five minutes' walk in every direction from the town center were fields of barley, dotted here and there with large farmhouses. Leh had the feeling of a village; everyone knew and greeted each other.

Over the last sixteen years, I have watched this village turn into an urban sprawl. Soulless, cell-like "housing colonies" have eaten into the green fields and spread into the dusty desert, punctuated not by trees, but by electricity poles. Flaking paint, rusting metal, broken glass, and discarded plastic rubbish are now part of the scenery; billboards advertise cigarettes and powdered milk.

For centuries, Leh was rooted in a sustainable economy. There was a dynamic balance between the urban and the rural, the one complementing the other. While some people made a living from trade with the outside world, most economic activity was based on local resources. Now development is transforming Leh into a center with very different economic foundations. The building of a road connecting the town with the outside world has hooked Ladakh up to the global macroeconomy and concentrated local economic activity in the capital. All the elements of modern living have been introduced there: electricity, the only gas station, the government, paid employment, the only hospital and cinema hall, the better schools, the two banks, even a football stadium. Development in Ladakh, as elsewhere, has worked like a whirlpool, pulling people relentlessly into the center. In the last sixteen years, the population of Leh has almost doubled, and the rural population has diminished as young people move to the city in search of jobs and education.

Cramming ever more people into such a small space causes many problems. In summer, the streets of Leh are crowded with stop-and-go traffic, the air choked with diesel fumes. Traditional courtesies give way to the pushing and shoving of modern urban life. People live in closer physical proximity to each other, but a distance develops between them. The political and economic structures that encouraged mutual aid and interdependence in the village have broken down; in time of illness or other need, a person in Leh is more likely to seek help from relatives in the village than from the strangers on the other side of the wall in the next apartment. Accommodation is cramped—often no more than two small rooms for a family of eight, without a bathroom or kitchen.

Norbu was brought up in his family house in the village of Stok: a three-floor building with whitewashed walls and carved balconies. Frescoes decorate the front rooms, which look out on fields lined with poplar trees and a glacial stream. To one side lies the village monastery; to the other, the royal palace.

Now Norbu lives by himself in one small room in Leh. Through the single window he can see a corner of a dusty football field, a barbed wire fence, electric poles, and a tangle of broken wires. Nearby, a crumbling wall, which serves as a public urinal, is set with broken glass to keep the animals away.

It was not entirely Norbu's own choice that he should leave his village and go to Leh—though no one compelled him to do it. It was more the result of the overwhelming pressures of modernization that draw individuals into urban centers. His education had prepared him for work in the modern sector, and all the jobs were in Leh. He was no longer qualified, either practically or psychologically, to work as a farmer.

Today's centralized economy is dependent on the use of large quantities of energy, and leads to a higher consumption of resources in general. Enormous investments in networks of new roads encourage a dependence on products from farther and farther away. In Leh these days, people provide almost nothing for themselves; food, clothing, and building materials all have to be transported into town —in a constant caravan of polluting trucks—in some cases from as far away as the south of India. Even water has to be "imported," often at the expense of the surrounding countryside, where essential irrigation supplies are being reduced. As a consequence, the age-old system of rotational sharing is breaking down.

People have almost no information about the potential health hazards of the new imported products. Many Ladakhis now bake their bread on scraps of asbestos, and I have even seen pesticide tins being used for salt shakers. Seventy percent of the pesticides used in India are either banned or severely restricted in the West; in Ladakh, despite the fact that there are almost no pests, farmers are encouraged to use BHC, which is more potent than DDT. Once, when I tried to explain to some Ladakhi friends that the butter they were using contained formaldehyde and was bad for their health, they were astonished. They could not believe that it would be sold in the shops and that so many people would be eating it if it was really so harmful.

Waste of any kind was unknown in the traditional village, but in Leh there is no means of recycling. Piles of rubbish accumulate, from leftover scraps of food to the plastic, glass, paper, and metal packaging materials required for long-distance transportation. Resources that were of real value in the traditional economy are now increasingly ignored.

Human waste, for instance, is no longer used to nourish the land; instead, it is becoming a problem, as scarce resources must be diverted in order to process it. As flush lavatories are built, energy is needed to raise precious water onto rooftops, so that gallons of it can be flushed away into miles of pipe and septic tanks. In the crowded conditions of Leh, leaking tanks have become a major source of contamination and have contributed to the recent increase in the incidence of hepatitis and other water-borne diseases.

In the modern sector, "diseases of civilization," which were almost unknown traditionally, are now increasingly common. These include cancer, strokes, and diabetes. Lack of exercise and increasing stress, coupled with a diet of processed foods high in fat and sugar, are largely responsible. In recent years, I have seen many of my Ladakhi friends become fat and unfit.

Medical care for tens of thousands of Ladakhis is now focused on a single hospital in Leh. As in most of the developing world, the end result is a poor imitation of Western medicine. There are some excellent doctors, but they are working in a system in which the odds are heavily stacked against them. The modern system is extremely capital and energy intensive; Ladakh's whole development budget and more would have to be pumped into the hospital for it to approach the standard of a Western one. As things are now, you have to wait a long time to see a doctor, the wards are crowded and understaffed, and medicines and equipment are in short supply. The provision of water is at best erratic, and sanitary arrangements are appalling.

Even this level of Western-style centralized health care, however, is enough to undermine the traditional system. The modern training for doctors ignores traditional methods, taking Ladakhis away from their own culture and resources. The amchi's way is based on having a lot of time: to learn the skills, to train an apprentice, to see patients, to prepare remedies. How can an individual amchi, who has to gather his herbs in the mountains before drying, grinding, and preparing them, compete with large pharmaceutical companies, which are part of the system subsidized by government? There used to be an *amchi* in almost every village; now there are far fewer, and young apprentices are fewer still.

Local agriculture is also being undermined. Subsidies for imported grain make it cheaper in Leh to buy a pound of wheat flour from the Punjab than from the nearest village. Rice, sugar, and other foods are also subsidized. As a result, it becomes "uneconomical" to grow your own food—an unimaginable concept within the traditional economy.

The modern economy plays havoc with common sense. In Leh these days, for instance, building with mud is becoming prohibitively expensive, whereas the relative cost of cement is falling. This is a good example of how Western-style development operates to undermine local systems. It seems impossible that a heavy and processed material that has to be transported over the Himalayan mountains can compete with mud, free and abundant, there for the taking. And yet that is exactly what is happening.

In the modern sector, land becomes a commodity with a monetary value. As people crowd together, the space allotted to them gets smaller, and land, which had never previously cost money, becomes more and more expensive. To make mud bricks, instead of simply digging up the land around your house, you have to travel ever farther from the spreading urban area and pay hard cash—for the mud itself, for the labor to make the bricks, and for the truck to haul them back into the city. Time now means money, and this becomes another disadvantage of using mud, since building in mud is slower. What is more, as mentioned earlier, the majority of "educated" people have not learned how to build a house, and the engineers work with cement and steel. As a consequence, the skills required to build with mud become ever more scarce, and thus more expensive. There is a psychological dimension as well: people are afraid of seeming backward—and everything traditional is beginning to be seen that way. They want to live in a modern house. A mud house is bad for the image.

In addition to food and building materials, the third basic need—

*Winter in Sankar village. The houses' thick adobe
walls serve to moderate the extreme climate.*

clothing—is being affected by the new economy. The traditional woolen clothing is being replaced by synthetic fibers, or even imported wool. It is becoming too expensive to wear a homespun robe, which previously had cost nothing.

I have watched a whole range of different pressures—all operating at the same time—pull the Ladakhis away from their own resources. The reasons are extremely complex and have to do with the systemic transformation of a whole way of life. However, it is very clear that the pull to the center is to a great extent a direct consequence of deliberate planning. The West's addiction to economic growth puts pressure on others to "develop," and in order to create the conditions for development, governments expend vast resources to restructure society. Everywhere, the underlying infrastructure—from centralized energy production to Western, urbanizing education—is essentially the same. And so, too, are the consequent problems.

CHAPTER FOURTEEN

A PEOPLE DIVIDED

Fashionism will give rise to proudness and less fellow feeling.
From an essay on change in Ladakh—Norbu, age ten

My first year in Ladakh, I was trekking from Chilling to the Markha Valley with a friend. We came to an extremely difficult part of the path, where there was a precipitous drop of hundreds of feet to the river below. An old man with a walking stick came surefootedly from the other direction. We greeted each other and walked on, as it was an impossible place to stand. My progress was painfully slow, and after about ten minutes, I heard the old man calling me. He had reached the end of the difficult section of the path and evidently noticed the trouble I was having. He retraced his steps, all the way back to where I was, to give me his walking stick. "You probably need this more than I do," he said with a smile. Now, when I get on the bus in the crowded station in Leh, I have to fight my way on board, and even old men try to push their way ahead of me.

In the traditional economy, you knew that you had to depend on other people, and you took care of them. But in the new economic system, the distance between people has increased so that it now appears that you no longer need one another. Ultimately, of course, you do, but no longer so directly as families, friends, and neighbors. Now your political and economic interactions take a detour via an anonymous bureaucracy. The fabric of local interdependence is disintegrating, and so too are traditional levels of tolerance and cooperation.

This is particularly true in the villages near Leh, where disputes and acrimony within close-knit communities and even families have dramatically increased in the last few years. In Skara village I have seen heated arguments over the allocation of irrigation water, a procedure that had previously been managed smoothly within a cooperative framework.

As mutual aid is replaced by a dependence on faraway forces, people begin to feel powerless to make decisions over their own lives. At all levels, passivity, even apathy, is setting in; people are abdicating personal responsibility. In the traditional village, repairing irrigation canals was a task shared by the whole community. As soon as a channel developed a leak, groups of people would start working away with shovels patching it up. Now, people see it as the government's responsibility, and will let a channel go on leaking until the job is done for them. The more the government does for the villagers, the less they feel inclined to help themselves. I remember talking to a government official about a hydroelectric plant that had been installed in the village of Nurrla. "I just can't understand it," he said. "They always looked after their old water wheels so well, but this thing they don't seem to care about. Earlier this summer, some rocks got into the turbine, but no one bothered to do anything about it—and now they don't have lighting."

Today, "development" is hooking people into ever-larger political and economic units. In the past, the individual had real power, since the units were small and each person was able to deal directly with the other members of the community. In political terms, a Ladakhi has now become one of 800 million, and, as part of the global economy, one of several billion.

The cultural centralization that occurs through the media is also contributing to a growing insecurity as well as passivity. Traditionally, there was lots of dancing, singing, and theater. People of all ages joined in. In a group sitting around the fire, even toddlers would dance, with the help of older siblings or friends. Everyone knew how to sing, to act, to play music. Now that the radio has come to Ladakh, you do not need to sing your own songs or tell your own stories. You can sit and listen to the best singer, the best storyteller. But the result is that people become inhibited and self-conscious. You are no longer comparing yourself to neighbors and friends, who are real people—some better than you at singing, but perhaps less good at dancing—and you are never as good as the stars on the radio. Community ties are also broken when people sit passively listening to the very best rather than making music or dancing together.

While I was waiting to meet a plane at Leh airport, I met Dawa and two of his friends. He was expecting a German tour group, and his friends were hoping to pick up some business. One of them ran a guesthouse, and the other was a trekking guide. They started telling me about a Hindi film that was currently being made in Ladakh. They had obviously spent hours around the set and had managed to get autographs, which they proudly showed me. Dawa was very funny imitating the heroine's high-pitched voice. They had picked up on every mannerism, every last detail: the way the hero moved, how he held his cigarette, which brands of cigarette and whiskey he preferred. The glamor of the stars had made a deep impression. Our conversation made me feel very sad.

Later that day I had my weekly meeting with Paljor, who was helping me to transcribe folk songs. I told him about seeing Dawa and his friends in the airport. "Paljor, aren't you upset by how the young people are changing? Dawa seems so confused about who he is. He's beginning to behave like a macho character in the films." "I know," he said. "My younger son is going that way too."

As they lose the sense of security and identity that springs from deep, long-lasting connections to other people, Ladakhis are starting to develop doubts about who they are. At the same time, tourism and the media are presenting a new image of who they should be. They are meant to lead an essentially Western life-style—eating dinner at a dining table, driving a car, using a washing machine. All sorts of consumer goods are held up as prerequisites of civilized society; modern kitchens and bathrooms become important status symbols. The images are telling them to be different, to be better than they are.

Surprisingly, perhaps, modernization is leading to a loss of individuality. As people become self-conscious and insecure, they feel pressured to conform, to live up to an idealized image. By contrast, in the traditional village, where everyone wears the same clothes and looks the same to the casual observer, there seems to be more freedom to relax and be who you really are. As part of a close-knit community, people feel secure enough to be themselves.

As local economic and political ties are broken, the people around you become more and more anonymous. At the same time, life speeds up and mobility increases—making even familiar relationships more superficial and brief. The connections between people are reduced largely to externals. People come to be identified with what they have rather than what they are, and disappear behind their clothes and other belongings.

Perhaps the most tragic of all the vicious circles I have observed in Ladakh is the way in which individual insecurity contributes to a weakening of family and community ties, which in turn further shakes individual self-esteem. Consumerism plays a central role in this whole process, since emotional insecurity contributes to a hunger for material status symbols. The need for recognition and acceptance fuels the drive to acquire possessions—possessions that will make you somebody. Ultimately this is a far more important motivating factor than a fascination for the things themselves. It is heartbreaking to see people buying things to be admired, respected, and ultimately loved, when in fact it almost inevitably has the opposite effect. The individual with the new shiny car is set apart, and this furthers the need to be accepted. A cycle is set in motion in which people become more and more divided from themselves and from one another.

I have seen people divided from one another in many ways. A gap is developing between old and young, male and female, rich and poor, Buddhist and Muslim. The newly created division between modern, educated expert and illiterate, backward farmer is perhaps the biggest of all. Modernized inhabitants of Leh have more in common with someone from Delhi or Calcutta than with their own relatives who have remained on the land, and they tend to look down on anyone less modern. Some children living in the modern sector are now so distanced from their parents and grandparents that they don't even speak the same language. Educated in Urdu and English, they are losing mastery of their native tongue.

One of the most divisive factors is the way in which the roles of male and female become increasingly polarized as their work becomes more differentiated. One of the consequences of industrialization around the world is that the men leave their families in the rural sector to earn money in the modern economy; Ladakh is no exception. The men become part of the technologically based life outside the home and are seen as the only productive members of society.

My friend Sonam is a typical example. His widowed mother and his sisters are still in Hemis. A few years ago he married, only to leave his bride in the village, where he sees her about four times a year. Even when he brings his wife and children to stay with him, he works long hours away from the house and sees very little of them.

Women, for their part, become invisible shadows. They do not earn money for their work, so they are no longer seen as "productive." Their work is not recognized as part of the gross national product. In government statistics, the 10 percent or so of Ladakhis who work in the modern sector are listed according to their occupations; the other 90 percent—housewives and traditional farmers—are lumped together as "nonworkers." This influences people's attitudes toward themselves and others, and the lack of recognition clearly has a deep psychological impact. Traditional farmers, as well as women, are coming to be viewed as inferior, and they themselves are obviously developing feelings of insecurity and inadequacy.

Over the years I have seen the strong, outgoing women of Ladakh being replaced by a new generation—unsure of themselves and extremely concerned with their appearance. Traditionally, the way a woman looked was important, but her capabilities—including tolerance and social skills—were much more appreciated.

One day when I stopped to see Deskit, I found her sitting alone in front of the TV at ten o'clock in the morning. She was in the best room, furnished with a large, new vinyl sofa and armchair, but she was sitting on the floor. Her children were in school, and her husband was at work. I had known her in the village when she was a bit shy, but pretty and sparkling. She was still pretty, but the sparkle had gone. She was clearly unhappy and had grown quite withdrawn.

I had come to see her because an aunt of hers had told me she was not very well. Neither the aunt nor Deskit herself knew why she was so unhappy, since she seemed to have everything she could possibly want. Her husband had a good job as a doctor, her children were in the best schools in Leh, and their house was modern, clean, and comfortable. But the process of development had isolated Deskit, imprisoning her in a nuclear family, removing her from the larger community, and leaving her without meaningful work. It had also separated her from her children.

Despite their new dominant role, men also clearly suffer as a result of the breakdown of family and community ties. They are deprived of contact with children. When they are young, the new macho image prevents them from showing any affection, while in later life as fathers, their work keeps them away from home.

In the traditional culture children benefited not only from continuous contact with both mother and father, but also from a way of life in which different age groups constantly interacted. It was quite natural for older children to feel a sense of responsibility for the younger ones. A younger child in turn looked up with respect and admiration, seeking to imitate the older ones. Growing up was a natural, noncompetitive learning process.

Now children are split into different age groups at school. This sort of leveling has a very destructive effect. By artificially creating social units in which everyone is the same age, the ability to help and to learn from each other is greatly reduced. Instead, conditions for competition are automatically created, because each child is put under pressure to be just as good as the next one. In a group of ten children of quite different ages, there will naturally be much more cooperation than in a group of ten ten-year-olds.

The division into different age groups is not limited to school. Now there is a tendency to spend time exclusively with one's peers. As a result, a mutual intolerance between young and old emerges. Young children nowadays have less and less contact with their grandparents, who often remain behind in the village. Living with many traditional families over the years, I have experienced the depth of the bond between children and their grandparents. It is clearly a natural relationship, with a very different dimension from that between parent and child. Severing this connection is a profound tragedy.

Similar pressures contribute to the breakdown of the traditional family. The Western model of the nuclear family is now seen as the norm, and Ladakhis are beginning to feel ashamed about their traditional practice of polyandry. As young people reject the old family structure in favor of monogamy, the population is rising significantly. At the same time, monastic life is losing its status, and the number of monks and nuns is decreasing. This too contributes to population increase.

Interestingly, a number of Ladakhis have linked the rise in birth rates to the advent of modern democracy. "Power is a question of votes," Sonam Rinchen put it recently, meaning that in the modern sector, the larger your group, the greater your access to power. Competition for jobs and political representation within the new centralized structures is increasingly dividing Ladakhis. Ethnic and religious differences have taken on a political dimension, causing bitterness and enmity on a scale hitherto unknown.

This new rivalry is one of the most painful divisions that I have seen in Ladakh. Ironically, it has grown in proportion to the decline of traditional religious devotion. I have already mentioned how, when I first arrived, I was struck by the mutual respect and cooperation between Buddhists and Muslims. But within the last few years growing competition has actually culminated in violence. Earlier there had been individual cases of friction, but the first time I noticed any signs of group tension was in 1986, when I heard Ladakhi friends starting to define people according to whether they were Buddhist or Muslim. In the following years, there were signs here and there that all was not well, but no one was prepared for what happened in the summer of 1989, when fighting suddenly broke out between the two groups. There were major disturbances in Leh bazaar, four people were shot dead by police, and much of Ladakh was placed under curfew.

Since then open confrontation has died down, but mistrust and prejudice on both sides continue to mar relations. For a people unused to violence and discord, this has been a traumatic experience. One Muslim woman could have been speaking for all Ladakhis when she tearfully told me, "These events have torn my family apart. Some of them are Buddhists, some are Christian, and now they are not even speaking to each other."

The immediate cause of the disturbances was the growing perception among the Buddhists that the Muslim-dominated state government was discriminating against them in favor of the local Muslim population. The Muslims for their part were becoming anxious that as a minority group they had to defend their interests in the face of political assertiveness by the Buddhist majority. However, the underlying reasons for the violence are much more far-reaching. What is happening in Ladakh is not an isolated phenomenon. The tensions between the Muslims of Kashmir and the Hindu-dominated central government in Delhi, the Hindus and the Buddhist government in Bhutan, and the Buddhists and the Hindu government in Nepal, along with countless similar disturbances around the world, are, I believe, all connected to the same underlying cause. The present development model is intensely centralizing, pulling diverse peoples from rural areas into large urban centers and placing power and decision making in the hands of a few. In these centers, job opportunities are scarce, community ties are broken, and competition increases dramatically. Young men in particular, who have been educated for jobs in the modern sector, find themselves engaged in a struggle for survival. In this situation, any religious or ethnic differences quite naturally become exaggerated and distorted. In addition, the group in power inevitably has a tendency to favor its own kind, and the rest often suffer discrimination.

In developing countries, people recognize that modernization is exacerbating—or even creating—ethnic rivalry; but they tend to think of this as the necessary price of "progress." They believe that only by creating a society that is entirely secular can this rivalry be resolved. Westerners, on the other hand, often assume that ethnic and religious strife is increasing because modern democracy liberates people, allowing old prejudices and hatreds to surface. If there was peace earlier, they assume that it was only the result of oppression.

It is easy to understand why people believe that violence is the result of cultural or religious differences, why they lay the blame at the feet of tradition rather than modernity. Certainly, ethnic tension is a phenomenon that predates colonialism and modernization. But after sixteen years of firsthand experience on the Indian subcontinent, I am convinced that "development" not only exacerbates existing tensions but in many cases actually creates them. Development causes artificial scarcity, which inevitably leads to greater competition, and puts pressure on people to conform to a standard Western model that they simply cannot emulate. Most people cannot be blonde and blue-eyed and do not live in two-car families. Yet this is the image that is held up as the ideal in our "global village."

To strive for such an ideal is to reject one's own culture and roots—in effect to deny one's own identity. The resulting alienation gives rise to resentment and anger, and lies behind much of the violence and fundamentalism in the world today. Even in the industrialized world we are victimized by stereotyped media images, but in the Third World, where the gulf between reality and the Western ideal is so much wider, the sense of desperation is that much more acute.

PART THREE

LEARNING FROM LADAKH

CHAPTER FIFTEEN

NOTHING IS BLACK,
NOTHING IS WHITE

*I wonder Mr. Gandhi did not go up to Ladakh; he would have
found here nearly all his heart craves.*
Major M. L. A. Gompertz, *Magic Ladakh,* 1928

In the preceding pages I have tried to give an overview of both the
traditional way of life in Ladakh and the forces of change in the modern sector. In talking about happiness, cooperation, and balance with
the land in the old Ladakh and contrasting it with alienation, social
breakdown, and pollution in the modern sector, my description
might well seem exaggerated, as though I have seen the traditional
life through rose-tinted lenses and painted the modern much too
black. But while it is true that much of what I have described in the
old Ladakh is positive and most of my description of the new looks at
negative changes, this is because I have primarily dealt with relationships and connections. I have tried to describe the shape and feel of
two contrasting ways of life rather than focusing on isolated factors.

Many individual aspects of the traditional culture were without a
doubt far from ideal: there was a lack of what we would consider basic comforts, like heating in the freezing winter temperatures. Communication with the outside world was limited. Illiteracy rates were
high; infant mortality was higher and life expectancy lower than in
the West. All of these are serious problems that I do not mean to
deny. But they are not quite as they appear when viewed from an out-

side perspective. Using Western yardsticks can be very misleading. Over the years, through intimate contact with Ladakhi society, I have come to see these limitations in a rather different light.

Traditional Ladakhi villagers did not consider it a hardship, as we would, to have to fetch water every day from a stream or to cook their food on a dung fire. Nor did they feel the cold to the same extent that we do. Once while I was hiking in late autumn with a nun from Hemis village, we crossed a stream that was so cold I screamed out in pain. My feet had turned bright red, and it took me fifteen minutes to recover. She, meanwhile, casually waded through the water, even pausing for a minute to look at something upstream, and looked quite perplexed when I asked her if she was not cold.

The limited nature of communication in Ladakh has also taken on a different meaning for me. The incredible vitality and joy that I experienced in the villages was almost certainly connected to the fact that the excitement in life was here and now, with you and *in* you. People did not feel that they were on the periphery; the center was where they were. Having the rest of the world through TV in your living room may not be as enriching as we tend to think. It may have just the opposite effect, in fact. The idealized stars make people feel inferior and passive, and the here and now pales in comparison with the colorful excitement of faraway places.

I certainly do not want to find myself in the position of defending illiteracy. There is no doubt that the Ladakhis now need to be able to read. In our society, being illiterate in effect means being powerless. Because of ever-larger political units, we have become utterly dependent on the written word. However, in the traditional culture, the scale was such that if you could speak, you were in a position to influence decisions. Even if you were illiterate your power to decide matters affecting your own life was actually greater than that of the average citizen in the West. Illiteracy in the traditional context was not what the term implies in the modern world.

Of all the factors that influence people's thinking about modern versus traditional society, none is more important than health and longevity. In traditional Ladakh people die from diseases for which Western medicine has found a cure, and infant mortality has been estimated to be as high as fifteen percent. Reducing disease and improving health are unquestionably important goals.

When one examines the reality of Western-style medical care in the Third World, however, things are not so clear. Surely it cannot be sensible to discard the traditional knowledge about local diseases and cures that has evolved over more than a thousand years. Nor can it make sense to introduce a poor imitation of a Western system that offers inadequate health care to the majority and cannot be sustained economically. Once again it is important to question the practice of addressing problems in isolation without regard for broader implications. For example, reducing infant mortality with no attention to population growth does not serve people's long-term interests. And while modern medicine may help you to live longer, if you find that you spend your later years cut off from your children and grandchildren, perhaps even crippled and incapacitated, longevity is perhaps not as important as we make it.

At the same time, the attitude to aging and death is all-important. In Ladakh, aging, as well as death, is regarded as part of a natural cycle. Often when I first see my Ladakhi friends after a period away, they will say, "You've aged a lot since I last saw you." It will be said quite matter-of-factly, like commenting on the change from winter to spring. It would not occur to people that I might not like to be told that I looked older. For the Ladakhis, there is no need to live in fear of the years; each phase of life has its own advantages.

Ladakhis do not believe that this life is your only chance. They see life and death as two aspects of an ever-returning process. Theirs is a culture that has come to terms with death; and their attitude is one of profound acceptance of inevitable change. Thus, even so traumatic an event as the death of a baby can have a different significance.

Just as there were considerable hardships in the traditional society, so development has brought real improvements. Obviously both the introduction of money and technology and the advent of modern medicine bring with them substantial benefits. Many Ladakhis are now much more comfortable than before. In addition, people enjoy being able to travel and to buy a wider range of material goods from outside. For example, rice and sugar, once luxuries, have become the food of every day.

Education is providing some with new and exciting opportunities, and for those who were socially disadvantaged traditionally, like blacksmiths, modernization promises the possibility of a higher position on the new social ladder. For young men in particular, the freedom and mobility that the modern world seems to offer are extremely seductive. The new ideals release them from bonds to other people and to place. It is no longer necessary for them to listen to their neighbors, parents, or grandparents. In fact, the modern ideal is the strong *independent* male.

Despite the very real problems in the traditional society and the equally real improvements brought about by development, things look different when one examines the important relationships: to the land, to one another, and to oneself. Viewed from this broader perspective, the differences between the old and the new become stark and disturbing—almost, but of course not quite, black and white. It becomes clear that the traditional nature-based society, with all its flaws and limitations, was more sustainable, both socially and environmentally. It was the result of a dialogue between human beings and their surroundings, a continuing dialogue that meant that, over two thousand years of trial and error, the culture kept changing. The traditional Buddhist world view emphasized change, but change within a framework of compassion and a profound understanding of the interconnectedness of all phenomena.

The old culture reflected fundamental human needs while respecting natural limits. And it worked. It worked for nature, and it worked for people. The various connecting relationships in the traditional system were mutually reinforcing, encouraging harmony and stability. Most importantly of all, having seen my friends change over the last sixteen years, I have no doubt that the bonds and responsibilities of the traditional society, far from being a burden, offered a profound sense of security, which seems to be a prerequisite for inner peace and contentedness. I am convinced that people were significantly happier before development than they are today.

And what criteria for judging a society could be more important: in social terms, the well-being of people; in environmental terms, sustainability.

By comparison, the new Ladakh scores very poorly when judged by these criteria. The modern culture is producing an array of environmental problems that, if unchecked, will lead to irreversible decline; socially, it is leading to the breakdown of community and the undermining of personal identity.

Again and again I have seen Westerners judge non-Western cultures as inferior because they tend to compare them with ideals rather than with any actual society. For instance, anthropologists compare class differences in traditional Ladakh to an ideal of perfect equality. They fail to remember that in their own society the gap between rich and poor is much larger than it is in Ladakh. Westerners also implicitly compare traditional cultures with the *ideals* promised by development and ignore the reality of what development has brought to societies around the world.

At my lectures in Europe and North America, people often ask the same question. Having seen pictures of the wide, uninhibited smiles of the Ladakhis and the beauty of the traditional art, architecture, and landscape contrasted with the meanness and spiritual poverty of the modern sector, they say, "How can the Ladakhis possibly want to give up their traditional way of life? They must want the change, there must have been some flaw in the traditional culture that makes them want to abandon it. It can't have been that good."

It is easy to understand why people make such assumptions. Had I not spoken the language fluently already in the first year, had I not been lucky enough to live closely with the Ladakhi people before the modern world entered their consciousness, I would almost certainly have thought the same way. But the Ladakhis I lived with were content; they were not dissatisfied with their lives. I remember how shocked they used to be when I told them that in my country, many people were so unhappy that they had to see a doctor. Their mouths would drop open, and they would stare in disbelief. It was beyond

*Can the Ladakhis' natural ebullience and joie de
vivre survive the pressures of modernization?*

their experience. A sense of deep-rooted contentedness was something they took for granted.

If the Ladakhis had been eager to adopt another culture, they could easily have done so. Leh was for centuries a center of trans-Asian trade. The Ladakhis themselves traveled both as pilgrims and traders, and were exposed to a variety of foreign influences. In many instances they absorbed the materials and practices of other cultures, and used them to enhance their own, but it was never a question of adopting another culture wholesale. If someone from China came to Leh, the result was not that the young suddenly wanted to put on Chinese hats, eat only Chinese food, and speak the Chinese language.

As I have tried to show in this book, the pressures that lead to cultural breakdown are many and varied. But the most important elements have to do with the fact that people do not and cannot have an overview of what is happening to them as they stand in the middle of the development process. Modernization is not perceived as a threat to the culture. The individual changes that come along usually look like unconditional improvements; there is no way of anticipating their negative long-term consequences, and the Ladakhis have almost no information about the impact that development has had in other parts of the world. It is only in looking back that any destructive effects become obvious.

An equally important factor in cultural breakdown is the sense of inferiority produced by contact with the modern world. Before, the Ladakhis were self-sufficient, psychologically as well as materially. There was no desire for the sort of development that later came to be seen as "need." Time and again, when I asked people about the changes that were coming, they showed no great interest in being modernized; sometimes they were even suspicious. In remote areas, when a road was about to be built, people at best felt ambivalent about the prospect. The same was true of electricity. I remember distinctly how, in 1975, a group of people in Stagmo village were joking and laughing about the fuss that was being made to bring lighting to neighboring villages. They thought it was a joke that so much effort and money were spent on what they took to be a ludicrous gain. "Is it worth all that bother just to have that thing dangling from your ceiling?" Two years ago when I arrived in the same village to meet the council, the first thing they said to me was: "Why do you bother to come to our backward village where we live in the dark?" They said it jokingly, but it was obvious that they were ashamed of the fact they did not have electricity.

Before people's sense of self-respect and self-worth had been shaken, electricity was not needed to prove that they were civilized. But within a short period I have seen the forces of development so undermine people's self-esteem that not only electricity, but Punjabi rice and plastic have become needs. I have seen people proudly wear wrist watches they cannot read and for which they have no use. As the desire to appear modern grows, people are rejecting their own culture. Even the traditional foods are no longer a source of pride. Now when I'm a guest in a village, people apologize if they serve *ngamphe* instead of instant noodles.

In the process, Ladakhis are starting to change their perception of the past. In the early days, people would tell me there had never been hunger in Ladakh. I kept hearing the expression *"tungbos zabos"*— enough to drink, enough to eat. Now, particularly in the modern sector, people can be heard saying, "Development is essential; in the past we couldn't manage, we didn't have enough."

For the reasons I have tried to outline, most Ladakhis now deem development necessary. And although the traditional society compares so favorably with the new, it was of course not perfect; there was certainly room for improvement.

But does development have to mean destruction? I do not believe so. I am convinced that the Ladakhis could raise their standard of living without sacrificing the sort of social and ecological balance that they have enjoyed for centuries. To do so, however, they would need to build on their own ancient foundations rather than tearing them down, as is the way of conventional development.

CHAPTER SIXTEEN

THE DEVELOPMENT HOAX

If Ladakh is ever going to be developed we have to figure out how to make these people more greedy. You just can't motivate them otherwise.

Development Commissioner in Ladakh, 1981

When I first arrived in Ladakh the absence of greed was striking. As the Development Commissioner observed, people were not particularly interested in sacrificing their leisure or pleasure simply for material gain. In those early years, tourists were perplexed when people refused to sell them things, no matter how much money they offered. Now, after several years of development, making money has become a major preoccupation. New needs have been created.

The messengers of development—tourists, advertisements, and film images—have implicitly been telling the Ladakhis that their traditional practices are backward and that modern science will help them stretch natural resources to produce ever more. Development is stimulating dissatisfaction and greed; in so doing, it is destroying an economy that had served people's needs for more than a thousand years. Traditionally the Ladakhis had used the resources in their immediate vicinity with remarkable ingenuity and skill, and worked out how to live in relative comfort and enviable security. They were satisfied with what they had. But now, whatever they have is not enough.

In the sixteen or so years since development first came to Ladakh, I have watched the gap between rich and poor widen; I have watched women lose their self-confidence and power; I have watched the appearance of unemployment and inflation and a dramatic rise in crime; I have watched population levels soar, fueled by a variety of economic and psychological pressures; I have watched the disintegration of families and communities; and I have watched people become separated from the land, as self-sufficiency is gradually replaced by economic dependence on the outside world.

When I saw a brass pot replaced by a pink plastic bucket, or yak-hair shoes thrown out in favor of cheap modern ones, my initial reaction was one of horror. But I would soon find myself thinking that I had no right to impose my aesthetic preferences or tell people what was good for them. The intrusions of the modern world might seem ugly and inappropriate, but surely they brought material benefits. It was only after several years that I began to piece these individual instances together and see them as aspects of a single process: the systematic dismantling of Ladakhi culture. I began to see the minor incremental changes in everyday life—a new pair of shoes, a new concrete house—as part of the bigger picture of economic dependence, cultural rejection, and environmental degradation.

As these connections became clearer to me, I grew suspicious of what is known as "development." This process of planned change, which was supposed to raise the standard of living through technological advance and economic growth, seemed to be doing more harm than good. I realized that the creation of greed was part and parcel of much broader changes. The development of Ladakh, as everywhere else in the world, required a massive and systematic restructuring of society that presupposed enormous and continual investments in "infrastructure": paved roads, a Western-style hospital, schools, a radio station, an airport, and, most importantly, power installations. All this involved not only the expenditure of exorbitant sums of money but also massive inputs of labor and administration. At no stage was it even questioned whether or not the result of these tremendous efforts constituted an improvement on what had existed before. It was like starting from zero, as if there had been no infrastructure in Ladakh before development. It was as if there had been no medical care, no education, no communication, no transport or trade. The intricate web of roads, paths, and trade routes, the vast and sophisticated network of irrigation canals maintained over centuries: all these signs of a living, functioning culture and economic system were treated as though they simply did not exist. Ladakh was being rebuilt according to Western guidelines—in tarmac, concrete, and steel.

As one of the last subsistence economies to survive virtually intact to the present day, Ladakh has been a unique vantage point from which to observe the whole process of development. Its collision with the modern world has been particularly sudden and dramatic. Yet the transformation it is now experiencing is anything but unique; essentially the same process is affecting every corner of the world.

As I begin to relate the changes in Ladakh to similar patterns of change elsewhere, I will inevitably be making some broad generalizations. I make no apology for this, because the process of modernization that I am describing is itself one enormous generalization—substituting a single monoculture and economic system for regional diversity and self-reliance.

Development works on the assumption that the introduction of cash is invariably an improvement. The more money, the better. But while this may be true for those dependent on the mainstream economy, it is certainly not true for the millions of people living within, or benefiting from, a subsistence economy—that is, a non-monetized economy based on a direct relationship with local resources. For these people, who are able to produce their own food, clothing, and shelter, there is a significant reduction in the quality of life once they relinquish their own culture and independence for an unstable monetary income.

The situation in Ladakh and the neighboring Himalayan kingdom of Bhutan vividly illustrates the shortcomings of defining human welfare only in terms of money. In each case, the standard of living is actually quite high when compared with most of the Third World. People provide their own basic needs, and still have beautiful art and music, and significantly more time for family, friends, and leisure activities than people in the West. Yet the World Bank describes Bhu-

*Ancient and modern houses. According to conventional
economic yardsticks, this is progress.*

tan as one of the poorest countries in the world. Because its gross national product (GNP) is virtually zero, the country is ranked at the bottom of the international economic order. In effect this means that no distinction is made between the homeless on the streets of New York and Bhutanese or Ladakhi farmers. In both cases there may be no income, but the reality behind the statistics is as different as night from day.

Whether in remote subsistence economies or in the heart of the industrialized world, there is clearly something wrong with a system of national accounting that sees GNP as the prime indicator of social welfare. As things stand, the system is such that every time money changes hands—whether from the sale of tomatoes or a car accident—we add it to the GNP and count ourselves richer. Policies that cause GNP to rise are thus often pursued despite their negative impact on the environment or society. A nation's balance sheet looks better, for instance, if all its forests have just been cut to the ground, since felling trees makes money. And if crime is on the increase and people buy more stereos or video recorders to replace those stolen, if we put the sick and elderly into costly care institutions, if we seek help for emotional and stress-related problems, if we buy bottled water because drinking water has become so polluted, all these contribute to the GNP and are measured as economic growth.

The situation has become quite absurd: rather than eating a potato grown in your own garden, it is better for the economy if you buy a potato grown on the other side of the country, which has been pulverized, freeze-dried, and reconstituted into brightly colored potato balls. Consuming in this way, of course, means more transportation, more use of fossil fuels, more pollution, more chemical additives and preservatives, and more separation between producer and consumer. But it also means an incremental increase in GNP, and is therefore encouraged.

This one-dimensional view of progress, widely favored by economists and development experts, has helped to mask the negative impact of economic growth. Moreover, it has blinded us to the value of locally based subsistence economies. This has led to a grave misunderstanding of the situation of the majority of people on earth today—the millions in the rural sector of the Third World—and has disguised the fact that development programs, far from benefiting these people, have in many cases served only to lower their standard of living.

Farmers who had previously grown a variety of crops and kept a few animals to provide for themselves—either directly or through the local economy—are now encouraged to grow a single cash crop for distant markets. In this way they become dependent on forces beyond their control—huge transportation networks, oil prices, and the fluctuations of international finance. Over the course of time, inflation obliges them to produce more and more, so as to secure the income that they now need in order to buy what they used to grow themselves.

Since even the most meager salary or payment in the cash economy is regarded as an improvement, cash cropping and the consequent increase in trade and transport appear unequivocally beneficial. In fact conventional development often results in the creation of poverty, as rural populations are lured away from the land into urban slums. Increasingly, people are locked into an economic system that pumps resources out of the periphery into the center— from the nonindustrialized to the industrialized parts of the world, from the countryside to the city, from the poor to the rich. Often, these resources end up back where they came from as commercial products, packaged and processed, at prices that the poor can no longer afford.

As a function of the same process, development money flows freely into large-scale projects aimed at increasing market transactions. Silently, without public debate, billions of dollars are poured into building roads, dams, and fertilizer plants, all of which serve to reinforce the dependence on centralized systems and increased energy consumption. Yet when it comes to small-scale projects that truly promote self-reliance, such as village-scale hydroelectric installations or solar ovens and water heaters for the household, the question is immediately asked: "Can the people pay?" Nuclear reactors and big dams are heavily subsidized, while small-scale technologies based on renewable energy receive no significant support from any of the major aid agencies. One of the greatest scandals of development is that despite tremendous potential, not a single country in the developing world has managed to promote small-scale decentralized applications of solar energy on anything more than a token basis.

Throughout the world, the process of development has displaced and marginalized self-reliant local economies in general, and small farmers in particular. In the industrialized world, more than 90 percent of the population has been pulled away from agriculture. Now, the same process is occurring in the Third World, only much more rapidly, as rural subsistence is steadily eroded.

The same forces that push farmers off the land seek to replace them with the ever more capital- and energy-intensive methods of industrial agriculture. It is assumed that this shift from agriculture to agribusiness is necessary in order to increase yields, and that increased yields are in turn necessary to feed the growing global population. Industrial agriculture, however, has proved to be unsustainable. Its fertilizers and pesticides pollute the water and destroy the soil, and after an initial increase, yields tend to decline. In addition, monoculture makes the crop very vulnerable to destruction by a single pest, while chemical pesticides have tended to disrupt natural systems of pest control. Farmers in Ladakh who have been persuaded to use pesticides tell of a noticeable increase in pests!

Industrial agriculture is now eliminating the diverse range of seeds indigenous to specific environments and replacing them with standardized strains. Multinational corporations and large petrochemical companies are expropriating seeds, particularly from the Third World, and using the genetic information—which represents millennia of adaptation to local conditions—to create hybrids. These are then sold back to Third World farmers along with the chemical fertilizers and pesticides that they require. These hybrids often lack the ability to regenerate themselves, and farmers are forced into a cycle of dependence, buying new seeds and chemical inputs from the corporations that own and control them.

As the logic of industrial agriculture unfolds, it looks increasingly sinister. With the biotechnology revolution—the transplanting of "desirable" genetic traits from one organism to another—we are seeing scientific manipulation on a grand scale. As nature is adapted to meet the needs of industry the result is greater standardization and uniformity, and thus increased vulnerability.

The emphasis is not on human welfare but commercial gain. Despite the fact that much of the research was done with public funds, control of this technology is firmly in the hands of transnational corporations, which are now able to engineer plant, animal, and even human genes, to turn them into products that can be patented and sold.

Of course, people have been developing hybrids in one way or another since the beginning of agriculture. The *dzo* in Ladakh is an example of a crossbreed that is well suited to its environment. What is different about today's genetic engineering is that the hybrids it develops have no connection with living local ecosystems. Moreover, the genetic base of life is being manipulated without any clear idea of the long-term consequences. What we do already know is that these technologies erode diversity and unravel the web of biological interdependence.

The products of biotechnology promise to be better than nature: pest-resistant, drought-resistant, and high-yielding. But for how many years will the patented corn come up bigger and brighter yellow? And for how long will the tired soil sustain it? For people with unlimited faith in science and technology these are not matters of concern. A few years ago, when I expressed dismay about soil erosion in conversation with an executive from a major oil company, he responded: "Don't worry! We are working on new hybrids now. We won't need soil in the future."

With such devout faith in scientific advance, our vision has grown more and more specialized and narrow while our manipulations of the natural world have an ever more massive impact. Even the most capable scientists cannot predict the consequences of these manipulations as they spread through the web of life. Yet instead of becoming more cautious, we have allowed the time span between scientific discovery and market application to shrink to almost nothing.

It is not that scientific inquiry has no place or that technology cannot be useful, but the fact is that both have become linked to narrow goals of short-term profit and expediency and have been accorded an unwarranted influence in shaping our society. We are in danger of altogether losing sight of ethics and values.

So far I have used the terms "development," "modernization," "Westernization," and "industrialization" more or less synonymously, to refer to the same phenomenon—the interaction of a narrow economic paradigm with continual scientific and technological innovation. This process has grown out of the past centuries of European colonialism and industrial expansion, through which our diverse world has been shaped into an increasingly uniform economic system—one that is dominated by the powerful interests of the industrialized countries, the multinational corporations, and the Third World elite.

The promise of conventional development is that by following in the footsteps of the "developed" countries of the world, the "underdeveloped" countries can become rich and comfortable too. Poverty will be eliminated, and the problems of overpopulation and environmental degradation will be solved.

This argument, reasonable as it may seem at first glance, in fact contains an inherent flaw, even deception. The fact is that the developed nations are consuming essential industrial resources in such a way and at such a rate that it is impossible for underdeveloped areas of the world to follow in their footsteps. When one-third of the world's population consumes two-thirds of the world's resources, and then in effect turns around and tells the others to do as they do, it is little short of a hoax. Development is all too often a euphemism for exploitation, a new colonialism. The forces of development and modernization have pulled most people away from a sure subsistence and got them to chase after an illusion, only to fall flat on their faces, materially impoverished and psychologically disoriented. A majority are turned into slum dwellers—having left the land and their local economy to end up in the shadow of an urban dream that can never be realized.

How is it that this hoax is still being perpetuated? It is easy enough to understand why conventional development seems attractive to people like the Ladakhis, since it appears to offer enormous benefits at no apparent cost. They have no way of knowing, for instance, that their relationship with their grandparents is going to change because they have more money or a car. But why is it that the rest of us, who have seen the effects of development around the world, continue to perpetuate the myth that everyone is going to live the American Dream? To some extent, at least, the answer is to be found in vested interests. Members of the Third World elite routinely "cream off" development money, and a primary goal of industrialized countries is to create a market for their own expertise and products.

But there is more to it than that. After all, development is not exclusively in the hands of people with narrow, selfish motives; plenty of development professionals would genuinely like to see a more equitable and ecological kind of development. And yet the drift of development today remains essentially the same as it always has been. While *self-help, self-reliance,* and *sustainability* have become quite fashionable terms, the level of dependence and debt is escalating, and money continues to be directed primarily to large-scale projects that are socially and environmentally destructive.

Development planners can pretend that everyone will be able to live like a New Yorker as long as they ignore the fact that natural resources are limited. There has been a long-standing debate on this point between economists and environmentalists. Economists and technical optimists assume that we will be able to invent our way out of any resource shortage, that science will somehow stretch the earth's bounty ad infinitum. Such a view is a denial of the fact that the natural world has limits that are beyond our power to change and conveniently circumvents the need for a redistribution of wealth. A change in the global economy is not necessary if you believe there will always be more and more to go around. The peoples of the Third World have only to get "educated" and step into the global market to one day live exactly as their big brothers in the industrialized countries.

According to this way of thinking, poverty and overpopulation are the major problems in the world today, and economic development is held up as the solution. The truth is, however, that while these problems are fundamental and serious, they are to a great extent the products of conventional development. The urbanization and industrialization that development promotes, together with the consequent neglect of agriculture and the rural economy, have created destitution on a massive and unprecedented scale. My experience in Ladakh suggests that a variety of economic and psychological pressures have a bearing on population growth, but that the disruption of people's direct relationship to local resources is the principal cause. In fact, demographers recognize that it is *after* contact with the modern world that population levels shoot up.

The escalating environmental problems and increasing levels of Third World debt and hunger should be seen as indications that something is wrong with the present development model. However, while there has been intense debate on the subject in recent years, it does not go far enough. At almost every level, from multilateral agencies to small grass-roots organizations, there is talk of a major policy shift toward support for more ecological and sustainable projects. But perhaps because development is not understood as the broad systemic process that it is, many of its destructive consequences continue to be dismissed as "side effects" or somehow attributed to the natural state of affairs. Most of the literature on sustainable development does not directly tackle the underlying causes behind social and ecological destruction.

Even small, idealistic organizations tend to ignore the root problems, often pulling more and more people into dependence on the macroeconomy rather than supporting local diversification and real self-reliance. Just as importantly, by not questioning the present educational model, these organizations show that they do not understand the need for a fundamental change in the direction of development. The majority still actively supports an education that trains people to become Westernized urban consumers.

Similarly, even those groups that work with small-scale technologies based on renewable energy tend to imply that this option is for the rural poor alone and that the "real," heavily subsidized development has to go on side by side. Most of the appropriate-technology literature, which typically shows people crouching next to some bits of rusty metal, is an indication of this attitude. Furthermore, the great majority of appropriate-technology projects promote technology in isolation, without considering the broader economic and cultural context. Under these conditions, appropriate technology is doomed to fail. Yet until it is properly resurrected, there is no hope of sustaining ecological and cultural diversity. Instead, the never-ending cycle of debt and dependence will continue, as developing countries compete for foreign exchange to acquire high-tech "efficient" technologies.

Born of a Eurocentric science and implemented by Westerners and Westernized elites, development is in the process of reducing all the diverse cultures of the world to a single monoculture. It is based on the assumption that needs are everywhere the same, that everyone needs to eat the same food, to live in the same type of house, to wear the same clothes. The same cement buildings, the same toys, the same movies and television programs find their way to the most remote corners of the world. Even language is becoming homogenized, since it is necessary to learn English to be part of the modern community.

The same yardsticks, originally developed for Europeans, are used everywhere. For instance, the indicators that determine how much a baby should weigh at a certain age, what the minimum room temperature should be, and what a healthy diet is, are applied universally. Western experts refer to both the people and animals of Ladakh as "stunted" because they are smaller than the global standard! The accepted levels for exposure to radiation, which were established for young European white males, are applied to all people regardless of age, sex, or size. The narrow and specialized outlook of some experts prevents them from seeing the broad implications of their work and the cultural insensitivity of their universal answers. When asked, at a recent symposium, about the vegetables they used to eat in Africa before we started exporting our seeds to them, a Swedish agricultural specialist answered, "They didn't have any. They used to eat weeds." To him the plants they ate did not have the same status as the plants that he was used to calling "vegetables."

Over the years in Ladakh, I have come to realize that the growing problems I have witnessed there have much more to do with modern industrial culture than with some sudden change in the Ladakhis themselves. I now see that it is not human nature that is to blame when Ladakhi friends become greedy and selfish or start to throw rubbish into hitherto unpolluted streams; the roots of these changes lie more with the technological and economic pressures that are dividing people from one another and from the land.

This realization has helped me to see more clearly the pressures that conventional development is exerting in other parts of the world. All the disastrous trends that I have seen emerging in Leh as Ladakh modernizes have direct parallels with those taking place on a large scale in urban centers throughout India. The beautiful lakeside city of Srinagar is now overrun by rampant commercialism, and beset by air and water pollution, social unrest, and insecurity. In the last couple of years it has literally become a battlefield in a separatist war against Indian authority. Meanwhile, Delhi is becoming noticeably more polluted every year. Traffic is growing exponentially, and so are hacking coughs. Concrete suburban housing developments and grimy industrial estates are swelling the sprawl of what used to be a walled city. The water is no longer drinkable, the streets are no longer safe, the increasing level of violence and frustration is almost tangible. There is an alarming growth of domestic violence against women; crime and ethnic or religious conflict are chronic afflictions.

In the forty years since independence, India has been implementing a concerted program of industrial development. During this relatively brief period, population has more than doubled and poverty has escalated. The pressure of numbers and the abuse of natural systems have precipitated environmental breakdown. Development has benefited at most fifteen or twenty percent of Indians, while the majority have been impoverished and marginalized.

Returning each year to the West, I have become increasingly aware that the pressures of economic and technological change are bearing down even on our culture in a similar way; we too are being "developed." Today, even though only 2 or 3 percent of the population is left on the land, small farmers are still being squeezed out of existence; and even though industrialization has pared the family down to a small nuclear unit, our economy is still chipping away at it. Technological advance is continuing to speed life up, while robbing people of time. Increased trade and ever-greater mobility are furthering anonymity and a breakdown of community. In the West these trends are labelled "progress," rather than "development," but they emanate from the same process of industrialization that inevitably leads to centralization, social degradation, and the wasteful use of resources.

"Progress" has reached an advanced stage in many parts of the world. Wherever we look, we can see its inexorable logic at work—replacing people with machines, substituting global markets for local interdependence, replacing country lanes with freeways in Wales, and the corner shop with a supermarket in Germany. In this light, even the differences between communism and capitalism seem almost irrelevant. Both have grown out of the same scientific world view, which places human beings apart from and above the rest of creation; both assume that it is possible to go on stretching natural resources indefinitely—the only significant point of difference being how to divide them up.

Regardless of their political orientation, governments are locked into an economic system that thrives on increasing international trade. This trade receives heavy subsidies—in particular, to maintain and expand networks of communication and transportation. Swedish biscuits or New Zealand apples can only compete with local products in America or France because of an energy-intensive system laden with hidden subsidies and ignored pollution costs. The globalization of the economy marches under the banner of "free trade," and is almost universally considered beneficial. The people of Sweden hear only of the potential benefits of joining the European Community, while in Mexico the advantages of liberalizing trade with the United States go unchallenged. Publicity about the Uruguay Round of the General Agreement on Tariffs and Trade (G.A.T.T.) talks of the positive effects it will have on oiling the wheels of international commerce. Its antidemocratic and unjust effects—the delivery of massive and unprecedented economic control into the hands of powerful multinational companies, and the further reduction of the status of Third World countries within the world economy—remain hidden.

It is not strange that there is so little opposition to a unified global economy and so little publicity about its social and environmental disadvantages. The concept of unity has tremendous symbolic appeal; the ideals of universal harmony and coming together have been embraced by all major religious and spiritual traditions and have come to represent the highest goal of humanity. "One market" implies community and cooperation and the "Global Village" sounds like a place of tolerance and mutual exchange. There is almost no recognition that economic unification and technological uniformity are actually causing environmental destruction and the disintegration of communities. Rather than bringing people together, today's economy is increasing divisiveness and widening the gap between rich and poor. We are moving toward a massive centralization of economic and political power. National governments are handing over more and more control and abdicating responsibility in favor of supranational institutions like the European Community and the World Bank. Such organizations are ever further removed from the people they are supposed to represent, and incapable of responding to their diverse interests.

These political changes are in fact a reflection of an economic centralization that threatens to allow multinational corporations to outstrip governments in their influence and power. Such trends are extremely disturbing since these corporations lie outside the realm of democratic control. Organized labor and environmental pressure groups are no match for the mobility of giant corporations: they may struggle for years to help enact legislation that protects workers' rights or bans a certain toxic chemical, only to find that companies can relocate their operations to a part of the world with less stringent controls. This is the meaning of the free market for transnationals— freedom from constraint in their search for new profits.

Today, the global economy is powered by the relentless drive toward more exploitation of resources, more technological innovation, more markets, more profits. Monetary and psychological pressures are pushing people in the developing and developed parts of the world alike toward a blind consumerism. The motto is "economic growth for the betterment of mankind." Advertising and the media are tell-

Barbie and Rambo: role models for the new Ladakhi.

ing people what to do—in fact, telling them what to *be*: modern, civilized, and rich.

The rural peoples of the "Third World" gain a particularly distorted impression of modern life—one of ease and glamor, where everyone is beautiful, everyone is clean. They see the fast cars, the microwave ovens, and the video machines. They see people with vast amounts of money and hear figures about their fantastic salaries. Development around the world is now on "automatic pilot." Even where there are no planned programs in operation, development is kept going by one-dimensional images of modern life: images that do not include the side effects, the pollution, the psychological stress, the drug addiction, the homelessness. People who have been presented with only one side of the development coin are left vulnerable and eager for modernization.

CHAPTER SEVENTEEN

COUNTER-DEVELOPMENT

We are still reaching for the sky. In the developed countries people
are coming back down, saying, 'It's empty up there.'
Gyelong Paldan, at a meeting in Sakti village, 1990

As I watched the development process transform Ladakh, I began to realize how little information people had about the forces that were now shaping their lives.

In 1987, when I was talking about pollution with the head of the agricultural department in Ladakh, it became evident that he had never heard about the dying forests of Europe. He was shocked when I told him that almost half of the trees in Germany were sick or dead from acid rain.

My friend Yangskit Dolma had tears in her eyes as she said to me, "I hear that they have lots of bombs over there. When you go back to your country, please tell them to stop it. Please tell them that we don't want them."

A Kashmiri trader in Leh once told me proudly, "Our vegetables are much better than the local ones. We have at least seven different chemicals on ours."

Some years ago, a Ladakhi engineer came to see me, looking quite alarmed. "We must stop building greenhouses," he said. "Apparently they cause terrible damage. There has just been a big international meeting about it."

It goes without saying that these examples of apparent naiveté do not indicate a lack of intelligence; they are instead the result of a lack of information about industrial culture. How was Yangskit to know enough about life in the West to realize that I could not influence my society in the same way she could influence her own? And why should the Kashmiri trader question the value of insecticides and fungicides when he had been told only about their benefits?

Information about the long-term effects of everything from powdered milk for babies to a dependence on fossil fuels tends not to reach the least developed areas of the world. And the seductive images in the media and advertising that do arrive are not accompanied by warnings about toxic wastes, the erosion of farmlands, acid rain, or global warming.

People in the developing countries are also unaware that in response to such problems, many individuals in the industrialized parts of the world are seeking ways of regaining a balance with the earth. They do not hear that people who have been crowded into large urban centers, starved of real community and contact with nature, are beginning to question the assumptions behind "progress." They do not hear about the social and environmental side effects of the automobile and the fact that many who are dependent on it would prefer to use trains or bicycles, or to walk. Nor is it headline news that medical care in the industrialized countries is borrowing more and more from natural methods and that there is a shift away from a mechanistic interpretation of reality, toward a more spiritual one. It is not publicized that overwhelming ecological problems are forcing a change in the direction of agriculture in Europe and North America, that consumers in the industrialized world are willing to pay twice as much for unprocessed food free from chemical residues, and that even some governments are beginning to encourage farmers to move away from a reliance on chemicals, toward organic methods.

At the same time there is an information gap in the West about the realities of aid and development in the Third World. The majority of taxpayers are largely unaware of the impact of the projects that they are helping to fund. At most, perhaps, they hear of the building of roads and hospitals in impoverished regions, and assume that this constitutes an improvement. They tend to believe that they can best support poor countries by buying their products, without realizing that rural communities in the Third World might be better off in the long term growing food for themselves and local markets, rather than coffee, cocoa, or rice for markets in the West. Very little is heard of communities that are relatively independent economically and would prefer to stay that way, like the Chipko women, who hug the trees in the Himalayan foothills to prevent logging companies from felling them.

Moreover, although we in the West are increasingly well-informed of the potential hazards of industrial products, we are generally unaware of the lack of such information in the Third World. Experience of the unanticipated side effects of powerful drugs and chemicals, for instance, has caused us to be more wary of them. Without the benefit of such experience, people in the Third World tend to take far fewer precautions. Agricultural workers spraying fields with DDT are often quite unprotected, while medications that have been outlawed in the West are widely used—sometimes in terrifyingly high doses—even without a doctor's prescription.

In many industrialized countries, pollution and the unscrupulous marketing of dangerous and toxic products are kept somewhat in check, both through legislation and the vigilance of pressure groups. In developing countries, however, such controls are often woefully inadequate. The point was made dramatically clear during a meeting convened by the European Community in 1989, at which environmentalists were given the opportunity to present their view of the dangers of industrial agriculture to an assembly of policy makers and heads of industry. As they were spelling out the full horror of ecological breakdown in western Europe, a representative from one of France's leading industrial firms threw up his hands and exclaimed, "Yes, yes, OK! But just leave us the Third World!"

A concerted information campaign is urgently required if we want to avoid further destruction in the name of development and progress: an education program to correct the incomplete and misleading images of the industrial system that is propelling the world toward social and ecological breakdown. Rather than more development, we need what I call "counter-development."

The primary goal of "counter-development" would be to provide people with the means to make fully informed choices about their own future. Using every possible form of communication, from satellite television to storytelling, we need to publicize the fact that today's capital- and energy-intensive trends are simply unsustainable. Ultimately, the aim would be to promote self-respect and self-reliance, thereby protecting life-sustaining diversity and creating the conditions for locally based, truly sustainable development.

One of the most critical failings of conventional development is its reliance on a narrow, short-term perspective dominated by quantitative analysis. Counter-development would move beyond specialization and fragmented expertise to reveal the systemic underpinnings of industrial society. It would draw attention to family and community break-up; it would show up the hidden subsidies of a society based on fossil fuels; it would place environmental damage on the debit side of the economic balance sheet. In short, it would expose the escalating costs of our industrial way of life.

At the same time, counter-development would promote and popularize a new, wider, and more humane definition of progress. It would highlight some of the innumerable local initiatives around the world that are exploring more sustainable alternatives. It would point to the viability of traditional systems as well as bringing information about new trends in agriculture: about permaculture, biodynamics, and the booming movement toward organic methods of cultivation. It would report on bioregionalism and local economic systems, on the new, holistic approach to physics; it would publicize the windmills in Denmark and California, and the growing demand for acupuncture, homeopathy, and other nature-based systems of health care. It would make more visible the enormous interest around the world in environmental protection, soil conservation, and air and water quality.

The steps needed to stem the headlong rush toward unsustainable development can and should be taken on a massive scale, and should be implemented immediately. To combat the rapid spread of the monoculture, we need to meet it on its own terms: global, top down, fast-paced, and capital-intensive. To be effective, counter-development programs would require very substantial funding; opposing the Tehri dam in India or the felling of tropical rainforests can only be done with considerable effort and money. One effect of colonialism and development is that the great majority of people in the world who have power or influence speak one of a handful of European languages. As a result, educational programs to promote diversity can be undertaken relatively easily and quickly, making use of the same few languages to get the message out.

Although the concept of counter-development is not yet recognized as such, there are many efforts already underway that fall clearly within its parameters. Unfortunately, no development organizations I know of have such programs, but an increasing number of environmental groups are moving in this direction—for example, the network of groups whose pressure has led the World Bank to create an environmental department, the groups that are compiling literature on the dangers of nuclear energy to be distributed free of charge to nongovernmental organizations in Eastern Europe, and the group in the Philippines that has attempted to strengthen rural communities by bringing villagers into the city to meet with slum dwellers who can tell them about the problems associated with leaving the land.

Some of the most sophisticated of these efforts have been inspired by individuals from Third World countries who have spent long periods in the industrialized world and for whom the glamorized images of the Western lifestyle have been demystified. A good example is Nsekuye Bizimana, a Rwandan who spent more than a decade in Germany. In his book, *White Paradise, Hell for Africa?*, he describes how, at first, his idealized image of the West was actually reinforced. He was bowled over by it all: the fast food, the fast cars, the freedom and anonymity. Only after a couple of years did he begin to see beneath the surface—the loneliness and unhappiness, the injustice, and the waste. One by one, his illusions were shattered, and in the process he began to realize that his own culture had many positive qualities that the West had lost. Having experienced Western society from the inside, he became firmly convinced of the futility and inappropriateness of Western-style development for Africa, and started promoting indigenous, more self-reliant alternatives.

Other leading figures in the field have been influenced by similar experiences. They include Martin Khor of the Third World Network in Malaysia, Wangari Maathai in Kenya, Vandana Shiva and Anil Agarwal in India, and Pierre Rabhi in Burkina Faso. It is vital that more committed people in the Third World have the opportunity to spend time in the West, in order to see at first hand something of the dark side of modernization.

It is equally important for concerned Westerners to involve themselves in counter-development. Everyone with experience of Western culture can play a part, without the need for special expertise. As individuals, we can put pressure on governments and aid agencies, we can support grass-roots organizations working for self-reliance, and we can supply information needed to help local cultures resist destructive change.

Many people believe that any Western involvement in the Third World is wrong. In principle, this is, of course, a valid argument. But it conveniently sidesteps the fact that even while remaining at home, our lifestyle as Westerners—dependent as it is on the exploitation of other parts of the world—inevitably has an impact far beyond our physical presence. Moreover, we have invaluable experience of industrial culture, which is needed in less developed areas. If we are not to be involved in the Third World, would we simply shrug our shoulders on hearing, for instance, that mothers feed their babies powdered milk mixed with contaminated water?

"But they've got to learn for themselves," people say. "They have to go through it, too." Countless times I have heard caring and concerned individuals express these sentiments. In effect, this is treating people in the Third World like small children: no matter how much you warn them of the dangers, you can't stop them from putting their fingers in the fire. Moreover, it is an attitude that helps to perpetuate, albeit unwittingly, the development hoax. "Going through it too" implies emulating a model that is not replicable; the resources are simply not there.

Truly effective counter-development is a necessary prerequisite to finding sustainable solutions to today's problems. Unless the consumer monoculture is halted there is no hope of preventing ever-greater poverty, social divisiveness, and ecological degradation. But counter-development is not itself enough. In addition to opposing technological uniformity, we need to actively support ecological and cultural diversity, by encouraging the fullest possible use of local resources, knowledge, and skills. In "developed" and "developing" parts of the world alike, agricultural self-reliance should be given a central role in the economy. Equal weight should be given to female perspectives and values; family and community ties should be nourished.

If our starting point is a respect for nature and people, diversity is an inevitable consequence. If technology and the needs of the economy are our starting point, then we have what we are faced with today—a model of development that is dangerously distanced from the needs of particular peoples and places and rigidly imposed from the top down.

We need to regain a balance between the local and the global. Even though the phrase "think globally, act locally" is mouthed frequently these days, the thrust of modernization is entirely in the direction of globalization. Local cultures and economies are disappearing at an alarming rate and taking animal and plant species with them. Finding a sustainable middle path would necessarily involve active steps toward decentralization. Since extreme dependence has already been created on both national and international levels, it would be irresponsible to "delink" economies and cut off assistance from one day to the next. We cannot, for example, suddenly halt our purchase of coffee or cotton from those countries in the Third World whose economies totally depend on such trade. But we *can* immediately begin supporting aid programs that will enable farmers to return to growing food for local consumption, rather than cash crops for export to the West.

Parallel to economic decentralization we need to decentralize the production of energy. Again, this ought to happen both in the West and in the Third World, but because the energy infrastructure of most developing countries is still relatively limited, the widespread application of solar, wind, biomass, and hydropower technologies in these regions would be comparatively easy. Until now, however, it simply has not happened. Instead, the West has pushed its own industrial model, based on large-scale, centralized power production. One of the most effective ways of turning destructive development into genuine aid would be to lobby for widespread support and subsidies for decentralized applications of renewable energy.

Truly appropriate technology would be far less costly than "high" technology—not just in purely economic terms but, very importantly, in its impact on society and the environment. It would be born of research in specific social and geographical settings, and be tailored to them, rather than vice versa. As anyone who has been close to the land knows, variations in wind, water, sun, soil, and temperature are significant even within very short distances. Just as brick-making in Ladakh varies from region to region, depending on the type of mud available, so small-scale installations adapted to local conditions are required if we are to make optimum use of available resources. This would entail a listening, intimate knowledge of nature—a very different approach from the heavy-handed ways of industrial society.

If development is to be based on local resources, knowledge about those resources obviously needs to be nurtured and supported. Instead of memorizing a standardized universal knowledge, children need to be given the tools to understand their own environment. In the process, the narrow specialization and urban orientation of Western-style education would give way to a broader, more contextual and ecological perspective. Location-specific knowledge of this kind would be holistic and specific at the same time. Such an approach would seek to perpetuate or rediscover traditional knowledge. It would build on centuries of empathetic interaction and experience with the web of life in a particular place.

Support for local knowledge ought to extend to all areas of education, including the natural sciences. To get beyond the Eurocentricity of modern-day science we need to promote research that is less centralized and more accessible to a broader section of the population. Instead of isolating variables under artificial laboratory conditions, emphasis would be placed on experimentation by local researchers in diverse cultural and ecological environments. Rather than maintaining elaborate high-tech seed banks, for instance, farmers would be encouraged to grow rare indigenous varieties, thus perpetuating living reservoirs of biological diversity.

Farming provides the most basic of all human needs and is the direct source of livelihood for the majority of the people in the Third World. Yet the status of the farmer has never been lower. At international economic summits, agriculture tends to be viewed as merely a "stumbling block" to agreement on more important issues. In fact, if present trends continue, the small farmer may well be extinct in another generation. It is imperative that we reverse these trends by giving agriculture the prominence it deserves and actively seeking to raise the status of farming as an occupation. A decentralized development path would offer immense benefits for small-scale agriculture. Small farmers would be better off if emphasis were placed on food production for local consumption, rather than on crops for export; if their products did not have to compete with products shipped great distances via subsidized transport networks; and if support were given to developing agricultural technologies appropriate for local conditions, rather than capital-intensive farm equipment suited to large plantations and agribusiness. They would also benefit if support were shifted away from the use of pesticides and chemical fertilizers to more ecologically sound methods.

Many of these shifts are already underway. Farmers' markets, which shorten the distance between producer and consumer, are springing up, while around the world thousands of individuals and organizations are exploring locally based, sustainable alternatives, often inspired by the proven success of traditional agricultural systems. Official support, however, still lags a long way behind. Although there are encouraging signs that governments are recognizing the need for a move toward organic agriculture, economic incentives continue to favor biotechnology and large-scale agribusiness. We urgently need to put support for small-scale, diversified agriculture at the top of the list of national priorities.

A decentralized development path would inevitably strengthen the position of women and help to reinstate a balance between male and female values. In industrial culture, power is vested almost exclusively in men. Science, technology, and economics—the cornerstones of this culture—have been male-dominated from their very inception. Development has had the effect of leaving women behind—both literally and figuratively—as their men go off to urban centers in search of paid employment. And even within the farming economy, women have universally been marginalized as a result of mechanization. A decentralized economy, by strengthening local ties, would make it easier for women's voices to be heard. Women would then no longer be at the periphery of decision making and economic activity, but at the center of it.

In much of the Third World today, families are still whole and strong. Children and the elderly live and grow side by side, providing mutual support and security. Even family bonds, however, are under attack from the powerful forces of Western-style progress, which are causing ever-greater divisions between generations. In order to reverse this trend we need to support the strong community ties on which emotionally healthy families and individuals depend. This in turn means supporting strong local economies.

Such economies are much more than utopian ideals; they have served admirably in many parts of the world for millennia. They tend toward a more equitable distribution of wealth than growth-oriented centralized systems, and are more responsive to the needs of people and the limitations of natural resources. By supporting their revival, we also would be helping to maintain cultural and ecological diversity.

Considerations such as these lie outside the parameters of conventional development thinking. Yet they are, of course, absolutely fundamental to the cause of human welfare. That, lest we forget, must surely be the ultimate goal of development. As the king of Bhutan puts it, the true indication of a society's well-being is not gross national product but "gross national happiness."

CHAPTER EIGHTEEN

THE LADAKH PROJECT

Ladakh is such a paradise. What a pity it has to be destroyed.
Tourist in 1975

During my first year in Ladakh, many of the tourists I met were fatalistic. They were sure that crime, pollution, and unemployment would be inevitable consequences of the area's exposure to the outside world. In their eyes, progress was a natural and inexorable process that could take only one form. But I could not agree. I felt sure the destruction I saw starting to occur was neither necessary nor inevitable. Rather, it was a result of specific policies and perceptions that could be changed. I was convinced another way must be possible.

Just at that time, I came across a copy of *Small Is Beautiful*, by the economist E. F. Schumacher, which strengthened my conviction that development need not mean destruction. I had seen how people in the modern sector were starting to buy imported coal and wood to heat their homes in winter. To them, of course, this seemed an absolute improvement over burning sparse supplies of animal dung to combat the severe winter temperatures. However, as was already becoming apparent, the problems with transporting these fuels across the Himalayas were immense and prices were rising every year. There was no way a family in the traditional subsistence economy could afford regular supplies throughout the winter; the only means of buying these fuels was to plug into the money economy of Leh. This was contributing significantly to the drift away from the land into the capital, creating a dependence on an inflationary economy based on nonrenewable resources.

I began writing letters to both the state and central Indian governments, pleading for policies that would build on the strengths of the traditional culture and promote the use of renewable energy. In 1978, after several meetings with the Indian Planning Commission, I requested and received permission to organize a small pilot project to demonstrate some simple solar technologies. Solar energy was an obvious choice since the region receives more than three hundred days of sunlight a year. The focus of the project was to find an effective way of heating the houses, but we also built a demonstration solar oven and a greenhouse. Fortunately, an elegantly simple solar technology for heating houses was available, named the Trombe wall after its French designer. We found that this system could be easily adapted to the traditional architecture and available materials. A double layer of glass is attached to the outside of a south-facing wall, which is painted black to absorb the sun's rays. The ceilings and other walls are insulated with straw.

The Trombe wall proved to be ideally suited to Ladakh. Mud brick is an excellent medium for absorbing and storing solar energy; and the rays of the low winter sun effectively heat the room, while those of the high summer sun barely touch the wall, keeping the room cool and comfortable. The whole system costs about three hundred dollars to install, or the price of one *dzo*. As the average heating bill can otherwise be as much as two hundred dollars a year for fossil fuels such as coal, the cost of the wall can be recovered in less than two heating seasons.

Before we built our first Trombe wall, many people were somewhat skeptical. Phuntsog Dawa, who later became the first person to try one, laughed at the idea. "Don't be silly," he said. "The heat will leak out as soon as you open the door." And when we were building his wall, the straw insulation was a source of great amusement to the masons, who called it "a home for mice." Since then, however, interest in Trombe walls and other solar technologies has been steadily increasing.

A Trombe wall solar space heating system on a private house in the village of Saboo.
Built by local craftspeople, it blends well with the traditional architecture.

During my first years in Ladakh, I was focusing on linguistic studies, but as I trekked throughout the region collecting folk stories, I
found myself involved in counter-development without realizing it.
Since I was the only outsider to speak the language, people all over
Ladakh were constantly asking me about life in the West. The young
in particular were clearly forming an exaggerated picture of the
modern world and, as a consequence, beginning to reject their own
culture wholesale out of a sense of shame. People were starting to
think of themselves as poor. I became increasingly aware that coun-
tering faulty impressions and providing more accurate information
about the West was a valid and useful role for a Westerner.

After countless informal conversations as well as frequent radio
interviews, in which I found myself having to defend Ladakh vis à vis
exaggerated impressions about the West, the concept of counter-
development gradually crystallized in my mind. Since theater was
traditionally a popular form of entertainment, it seemed an effective
way of reaching people. I started writing a series of plays with Gyelong Paldan, with whom I had worked on the dictionary. The first

A scene from the drama Ladakh, Look Before You Leap.

one, *Ladakh, Look Before You Leap,* sums up the essence of our work quite well.

Young Rigzin rejects the old culture and does his best to live the life of a modern Westerner. He refuses to eat Ladakhi food or drink butter tea. He ridicules his parents for being so "old fashioned," and takes to smoking cigarettes and driving around on his motor-bike. He and his friends spend their time and money at discos, dancing to loud Western music. He dresses in jeans, and wears designer sunglasses.

One day, his grandfather gets sick, and Rigzin persuades his parents to bring a Western-trained doctor, recently returned from America. He showers the doctor with questions about life in the Western world. But he is in for a surprise. "In America," the doctor tells him, "the most modern people eat something they call stone-ground wholemeal bread. It's just like our traditional bread, but there it's much more expensive than white bread. People over there are building their houses out of natural materials, just like ours. It's usually the poor who live in concrete houses. And the trend is to dress in clothes with labels saying '100% natural' and 'pure wool.' The poor people wear polyester clothes. It's not what I expected at all. So much that is modern in America is similar to traditional Ladakh. In fact, people used to tell me, 'You're so lucky to have been born a Ladakhi.'"

Five hundred Ladakhis crowded the auditorium in Leh for the play's première, which was a great success. Afterwards, local leaders, including Chhewang Phonsog, the development commissioner and highest-ranking official in the local administration, made speeches about the importance of cultural self-respect. But there were other reactions, too. Sonam Paljor was annoyed. "You have exaggerated," he said. "Things aren't that bad." Sadly though, some years later he said his own son had actually grown up to mirror the young man in the play.

Through the language, I came to understand the Ladakhi way of thinking and became quite integrated into the society. Watching Western ways transform Ladakh, I was able to see my own culture through different eyes. The waste and injustice of our capital- and energy-intensive life-style became more obvious to me. And for the first time I understood something about the high psychological and social price of a type of development that isolates people from one another.

I embarked on a series of lecture tours and seminars in Europe and North America. Describing the social and ecological balance of traditional Ladakh and how conventional development was eroding it, I was able to highlight some of the root causes of our problems in the West. I hoped that by giving Western audiences glimpses of a culture based on principles quite different from our own I could inspire them with the belief that a more humane and sustainable way of life was possible.

By 1980, my activities in both Ladakh and the West had grown into a small international organization called the Ladakh Project, which in 1991 became the International Society for Ecology and Culture. We seek to encourage a revisioning of progress toward more ecological and community-based ways of living. We stress the urgent need to counter political and economic centralization, while encouraging a truly international perspective through increased cultural exchange.

We also feel that a shift from ever more narrow specialization toward a broad systemic perspective—an approach that emphasizes relationship and context rather than isolated phenomena—is essential to prevent further social and environmental destruction. To get our ideas across, we run workshops and lectures and produce videos and publications for educational purposes, including a series of papers examining global trends in such key areas as energy, agriculture, and health. These materials, based on our experience in Ladakh, can serve as useful tools for promoting discussion on global issues. We have found that people generally open their minds to the questions Ladakh raises much more readily than they would if the examples came from closer to home. When I lecture in America or Great Britain, the Ladakhis' smiling faces and obvious contentment encourage a reassessment of even the most entrenched view of what constitutes progress.

In Ladakh, the Project brings information about the shift toward more ecological practices in the most "modern" areas of the world. We have made efforts to describe the search for sustainable ways of living in countries like Sweden or the United States, for instance. Ladakhis can then draw parallels between these trends and their own preindustrial practices.

Early on, in response to the demonstration Trombe walls, the radio programs and dramas, a group of concerned Ladakhis became interested in exploring a more sustainable development path. They represented Ladakh's leading thinkers, people of great integrity and dedication. Many of them had traveled outside Ladakh, received a modern education, and yet retained respect for the values of their traditional culture. In 1983, we officially registered as the Ladakh Ecological Development Group (LEDeG). With a current staff of forty, LEDeG has become the most influential nongovernmental organization in the region. Together with the Ladakh Project, LEDeG continues to develop and demonstrate a whole range of appropriate technologies and now receives many more requests than it can possibly fulfill. In addition to the Trombe walls, we have built direct-gain systems for space heating. Other solar technologies include ovens for cooking rice and vegetables and baking bread and cakes, water heaters—both simple batch and thermosyphoning systems—and greenhouses that allow people to grow vegetables throughout the winter.

We have also developed hydraulic ram pumps made by our own technical staff entirely from standard plumbing parts. These raise water using the power of gravity instead of imported petroleum. One of the first pumps we installed lifted water 150 feet to the top of Matho Monastery to the amazement and appreciation of the monks, who previously had to carry water up on their backs. Another project has been improving traditional water mills so that they not only grind grain faster, but also provide mechanical power for driving tools. Since 1989, in response to the increasing desire for electricity, the main focus of our technical program has been on microhydro installations for domestic lighting in the villages.

All these technological alternatives make sense economically, environmentally, and culturally. By encouraging a more human-scale and decentralized development pattern, they actively support traditional structures rather than destroying them. And they are not "technologies for the poor," only suited to the underprivileged. As we do our best to make clear, nonpolluting appropriate technologies based on renewable energy are *not* something second-rate, but highly effective and efficient solutions to the long-term needs of both developed and developing countries.

All our projects involve the participation of the beneficiaries. Before we install a turbine, for instance, the villagers themselves will have helped to choose a site, improved an existing water channel, and made a holding tank. One or two villagers then come to our workshop in Leh for six months to learn how to run and maintain the installation. After the turbine is in place, the village is responsible for building a small powerhouse.

LEDeG's headquarters is the Center for Ecological Development in the heart of Leh. Inaugurated by Indira Gandhi in 1984 and consecrated by His Holiness the Dalai Lama, it serves the purpose of bringing our work and the thinking behind it to the attention of Ladakh's decision-makers and visitors from abroad. It has generated considerable interest not only within Ladakh itself, but throughout the rest

The Center for Ecological Development in Leh.

of India. Visitors range from government officials, journalists, teachers, and tourists, to Ladakhis from all walks of life. Here Ladakhis can meet foreign tourists face to face and on equal terms. This facilitates real communication between the two cultures, demystifying the West and showing the Ladakhis how much value the foreigners attach not only to traditional Ladakhi culture, but also to the work we are doing.

The building itself is an example of how traditional Ladakhi architecture can be "updated" to meet changing expectations and needs. Part of the building is solar heated, and hot water is provided by solar water-heating panels on the roof. A small wind generator provides power for back-up lighting. In the garden is an array of solar cookers and dryers and also a solar greenhouse. All these technologies are in active use and are accompanied by written and graphic material explaining how they work and how they are built.

The Center houses a restaurant serving food cooked in our own solar ovens. In addition, there is an ever-expanding library of literature showing the worldwide interest in ecological issues and sustainable development. We also have a workshop where we produce almost all the appropriate technologies ourselves and hold training courses for villagers. In 1989 we started a handicrafts program that we hope will support local self-reliance and help prevent a drift away from the land. By producing handicrafts during the winter months when there is very little agricultural work, Ladakhis can earn money without suffering the social or environmental costs involved in abandoning village life. The fifteen thousand or so tourists who come to Ladakh annually are currently buying souvenirs that almost without exception are not made by Ladakhis or even in Ladakh. Visitors to the Center can watch the weaver, silversmith, and woodcarvers at work outside using traditional handmade tools. Inside, tailors, embroiderers, and painters train young Ladakhis to make *thanka*s and wool *goncha*s.

We also have a broad-based educational program that includes radio shows on ecodevelopment and regular publications, one of which was the first book in Ladakhi on ecology. Frequent meetings, workshops, and seminars are a central part of our educational work. In 1986 and 1989, we organized international conferences that sought to bring to the attention of the Ladakhis the experiences of the more industrialized parts of the world. Other meetings range from informal groups of villagers discussing uses for their greenhouses and solar ovens, to hundreds of farmers from the entire region coming together to explore the future of agriculture in Ladakh. We also organized a series of seminars in which leaders from the Buddhist and Muslim communities sought ways to avoid communal friction. We have brought women together to discuss handicrafts, the dangers of baking on asbestos, and the all-important topic of agriculture.

Agriculture—the basis of the traditional economy—is threatened by food subsidies and cash-cropping, by the drift away from the land, and by the introduction of chemical fertilizers and pesticides. Many Ladakhis have come to believe that farming is a "primitive" occupation, and those who do farm believe it is "modern" to use artificial additives, knowing nothing of the potential long-term damage to the soil or their health. Through our meetings and newsletters, we inform people of the growing appreciation for organic methods of farming worldwide and do our best to raise the status of agriculture.

The village meetings often involve lively debate. At an agriculture seminar in Sakti, for instance, one young speaker vehemently opposed the notion that the youth were both ignorant and contemptuous of traditional farming practices. While he was talking, an older man interrupted: "Sure! Ask them to saddle a horse, they put it on backwards. Ask them to yoke a *dzo,* they run away scared. They buy expensive rubber boots that fall apart before you get to the top of the pass. We wore shoes we made ourselves that were warm and comfortable, and carried needle and thread and could repair anything we needed to in a minute. We stood on our own two legs and knew how to make use of everything around us. That's what you mean by ecology, isn't it?" he shouted out to the LEDeG staff.

These programs are largely implemented by LEDeG with the help of the Ladakh Project. We also work with the Students' Educational and Cultural Movement of Ladakh (SECMOL). Founded in 1988, SECMOL seeks to involve young people in development and to explore alternatives to formal education. Part of our support for SECMOL involves introducing its leaders to like-minded organizations and individuals in the rest of India and Europe. We have arranged study tours for them, as well as for members of LEDeG, in which they learn something of the problems of the industrial world and see first-hand the responses that these problems are generating.

Over the years, our work has expanded, and there have been clear signs of progress. But all has not been easy. Since Ladakh is a militarily strategic zone, foreigners are not normally allowed to live or work there. By my second year, an article had appeared in the *Hindustan Times* describing me as "a mysterious woman who has picked up the language in a suspiciously short time," hinting at some sinister motive for my presence in Ladakh. Despite continued high-level government backing, including personal meetings with and letters of support from prime ministers and state governors, several intelligence officers remained convinced I was a C.I.A. agent collecting information about this sensitive border area. More recently, I have even been accused of singlehandedly starting the communal riots that broke out in 1989 between Muslims and Buddhists.

In addition, our work met with skepticism from some of the young men just finding their way in the modern sector, particularly from those working in tourism. They were infatuated with all things modern and could not understand the need for our programs of environmental education. In their minds, we should be focusing our attention on providing immediate material benefits for the "poor farmers in the villages."

From an ideological point of view, our work has also been difficult. In trying to forge a fundamentally different development path, we have had few models to follow. We have struggled with some thorny issues: Could our efforts be doing more harm than good? Would Ladakh be better off without any development at all? Should development only come from the Ladakhis themselves with no outside involvement? How could Ladakhis organize effectively to face the changes brought by development, without eroding the strengths of the traditional culture? In answering these questions we have had to bear in mind the immense economic and psychological weight of the monoculture that has been bearing down on Ladakh for the last two decades. Around the world, Western interests are laying seige to nonindustrialized societies, making truly indigenous development a near impossibility.

The real life situation is extremely complex, calling for responses that appear contradictory on the surface. Thus there are many apparent paradoxes in our work. For example, we actually encourage contact between Ladakhis and Westerners, both in Ladakh and abroad, since real communication, such as the study tours we organize for SECMOL and LEDeG members, helps them gain a more balanced impression of the West.

Similarly, even though the Ladakh Project actively promotes decentralization, the sociopolitical reality is such that it makes sense to have a center in Leh. Whether we like it or not, that is where most decisions regarding Ladakh's future are made (insofar as they are made in Ladakh at all). Given our limited budget, this is also the most economical way of reaching the largest number of villagers.

Although I felt that solar heating could provide a clear improvement in living standards, I would not have considered it appropriate for an outsider like myself to introduce this technology had not other less sustainable heating methods—like coal and oil—already begun to disrupt traditional practices. Since they had, I felt that people should have the information to make a choice; higher standards of living need not mean abandoning economic independence or traditional values. With experience, however, we realized that demonstration was not enough. There was a need to actively support and propagate such alternatives, and to lobby the government to divert subsidies away from capital- and energy-intensive installations toward decentralized technologies based on renewable energy.

I certainly would not claim that the compromises we have made are unproblematic. Clearly, specific decisions and activities could have been different. But overall, I am convinced that we have been heading in the right direction, and there are encouraging signs that our efforts are bearing fruit. We have played a part in raising awareness of the need for a long-term ecological perspective on development, for a development based on self-reliance and self-respect. The terms "ecology" and "solar energy" are now widely used and understood throughout Ladakh, and there are a growing number of people who make the environment and Ladakh's future well-being a conscious priority. Among them are Tsewang Rigzin Lagrook, one of Ladakh's best-known horticulturalists, who has started something of a movement back to organic methods of agriculture—and this despite a loss in profit; Sonam Angchuk and Sonam Dorje of SECMOL, who made the courageous decision to forego prestigious careers in government service, and through their dedication managed to motivate large numbers of young people to devote themselves to social service; and Sonam Dawa, known throughout Ladakh for his exceptional integrity and foresight, who took the unprecedented step of retiring early from his high-ranking post in the state government to become LEDeG's director.

The Ladakhis still have an opportunity to avoid many of the pitfalls of conventional development, since a large proportion of the population is still economically independent. And our work, it seems, is striking a chord. Within Ladakh itself, development is now seen in quite a different light, while in the world outside, the story of Ladakh—the success of its traditional culture and its potential as a model of ecological development—helps to highlight some of the foundations necessary for a sustainable future for us all.

"ANCIENT FUTURES"

It seems to me that Western society today is moving in two distinct and opposing directions. On the one hand, mainstream culture led by government and industry moves relentlessly toward continued economic growth and technological development, straining the limits of nature and all but ignoring fundamental human needs. On the other hand, a counter-current, comprising a wide range of groups and ideas, has kept alive the ancient understanding that all life is inextricably connected.

At present, this is only a minority voice, but it is growing in strength as more and more people begin to question the whole notion of progress. The formation of Green parties and the rise in membership in environmental organizations indicate widespread commitment to environmental protection. Individual consumers are beginning to realize their power to bring about change in the economic system, and businesses are competing with each other to appear "environmentally friendly." Governments and major international agencies are under pressure to place the environment high on the political agenda.

We still have an opportunity to steer our society toward social and ecological balance. But if we are to do more than simply treat symptoms, it is important that we understand the systemic nature of the crises facing us. Under the surface even such seemingly unconnected problems as ethnic violence, pollution of the air and water, broken families, and cultural disintegration are closely interlinked. Understanding that the problems are interrelated can make them seem overwhelming, but finding the points at which they converge can, in fact, make our attempts to tackle them a great deal more effective. It is then just a question of pulling the right threads to affect the entire fabric, rather than having to deal with each problem individually.

The fabric of industrial society is to a great extent determined by the interaction of science, technology, and a narrow economic paradigm—an interaction that is leading to ever-greater centralization and specialization. Since the Industrial Revolution, the perspective of the individual has become more limited while political and economic units have grown larger. I have become convinced that we need to decentralize our political and economic structures and broaden our approach to knowledge if we are to find our way to a more balanced and sane society. In Ladakh, I have seen how human-scale structures nurture intimate bonds with the earth and an active and participatory democracy, while supporting strong and vital communities, healthy families, and a greater balance between male and female. These structures in turn provide the security needed for individual well-being and, paradoxically, for a sense of freedom.

The changes that we need to make can greatly enrich our lives. Yet they are often treated, even within the environmental movement, as sacrifices. The emphasis is on giving things up and making do with less, rather than recognizing how much we stand to gain. We forget that the price for never-ending economic growth and material prosperity has been spiritual and social impoverishment, psychological insecurity, and the loss of cultural vitality. We think of ourselves as "having everything," and are surprised when young people turn to drugs or strange gurus to fill the void in their lives.

Perhaps the most important lesson of Ladakh has to do with happiness. It was a lesson that I was slow to learn. Only after many years of peeling away layers of preconceptions did I begin to see the joy and laughter of the Ladakhis for what it really was: a genuine and unhindered appreciation of life itself. In Ladakh I have known a people who regard peace of mind and joie de vivre as their unquestioned birthright. I have seen that community and a close relationship to the land can enrich human life beyond all comparison with material wealth or technological sophistication. I have learned that another way is possible.

At the moment, the emerging global economy and the growing domination of science and technology are not only severing our connection to nature and to one another but also breaking down natural and cultural diversity. In so doing, we are threatening our very existence. In the natural world, diversity is an inescapable fact of life. We are just beginning to discover how important even the most "insignificant" insect or plant can be for our survival. The alarming rate at which we are eradicating species of plant and animal life has, in fact, become a major issue. Biologists are now corroborating the life-sustaining importance of species diversity, and some are speaking out about the danger of erasing it for the sake of short-term gain. Individuals throughout the world are organizing themselves to protect endangered species of plants and animals. In addition to safeguarding the future of wild animals, people are now breeding threatened strains of goats, sheep, ponies, and other domestic animals. Some apple farmers are choosing to propagate traditional local varieties before they are all replaced by a single hybrid such as Golden Delicious.

In a modern setting it is easy to believe that economic development has increased diversity. Efficient transportation and communication bring together a vast array of foods and products from different cultures. However, the very system that facilitates these multicultural experiences is helping to erase them and to eliminate local cultural differences throughout the world. Lingonberry and pineapple juice are giving way to Coca Cola, woolen robes and cotton saris to blue jeans, yaks and highland cattle to Jersey cows. Diversity does not mean having the choice between ten different kinds of blue jeans all made by the same company.

Cultural diversity is as important as diversity in the natural world and, in fact, follows directly from it. Traditional cultures mirrored their particular environments, deriving their food, clothing, and shelter primarily from local resources. Even in the West today, there are still remnants of local adaptation to diversity. In the American Southwest, you find flat-roofed adobe houses, which are ideally suited to the extremes of the desert climate, while in New England, the houses are made of wood and have pointed roofs designed to shed the rain and snow. The cuisines of different cultures still reflect local food sources, from the olive oil prevalent in Mediterranean cooking to the oatmeal and kippered herring on the Scotsman's breakfast table.

Without retreating into cultural or economic isolationism, we can nourish the traditions of our own region. A true appreciation of cultural diversity means neither imposing our own culture on others, nor packaging, exploiting, and commercializing exotic cultures for our own consumption.

One of the most effective ways of reviving cultural differences would be to lobby for a reduction in unnecessary trade. At the moment, our taxpayers' money is going to expand transport infrastructures and to increase trade for the sake of trade. We are transporting across whole continents a vast range of products, from milk to apples to furniture, that could just as easily be produced in their place of destination. What we should be doing instead is reinforcing and diversifying local economies. By reducing and eliminating subsidies for transportation, we would cut waste and pollution, improve the position of small farmers, and strengthen communities in one fell swoop.

What exactly is "local," and what is "necessary" as opposed to "unnecessary" trade, are issues that cannot be defined in absolute terms. But the crucial point is that the *principle* of heavily subsidized international trade is one that needs critical reassessment—not with the goal of encouraging protectionism, but so as to allow for the sustainable and equitable use of natural resources worldwide. It is in robust, local-scale economies that we find genuinely "free" markets; free of the corporate manipulation, hidden subsidies, waste, and immense promotional costs that characterize today's global market.

The trend toward a globalization of the market not only concentrates power and resources in ever-fewer hands, but contributes directly to ever-greater dependence on urban centers. Even though the numbers of people living in many Western cities may actually be falling, the pull to the center is increasing. Commuters are travelling farther and farther, while whole regions suffer severe decline as economic and political power is increasingly focused in a few large cities. Living and working outside the reach of these centers is becoming increasingly difficult.

It is often said that there are too many people and not enough land for a demographic shift into rural areas. But in many unseen ways, today's centralized systems take up much more space. The relationship between the vast urban centers of today and their physical requirements is analogous to the way we use more land the higher up on the food chain we eat. A beef cow does not take up nearly as much room in itself as a vegetable garden, but when you take into account the fields of grain to feed the cow, the water to irrigate the fields, and the land that dried up because of the diversion of that water, it is clear that a cow actually takes up much more land. A large city takes up less physical space than the same population dispersed into small communities, but it lives higher on the energy chain; and per capita consumption in the cities is also higher. The freeways, the transport, the used-car lots, the oil fields, the food-processing plants, the pollution of air, water, and land mean that contemporary urban centers use more resources and ultimately more space than decentralized communities closer to nature.

The process of decentralization would involve a succession of changes in the whole socioeconomic system. It is important to remember, however, that we are not talking about dismantling a static entity but rather about steering in the direction of change. The scale of our society is growing year by year, and the logic of centralization is progressively being carried to new extremes. The pace is such that we would need to actually implement plans for decentralization simply to stay where we are now. That alone would be a significant achievement.

The need to belong to a group is in itself an important reason for human-scale social units. Here we can learn directly from Ladakh, where families are large, but communities small. Children are nurtured by people of different generations, benefiting particularly from the special bond with their grandparents. Though the relationships in this larger family are close, they are not so intense as those of the nuclear family. Each individual is supported in a web of intimate relationships, and no one relationship has to bear too much weight. In Ladakh, I have never observed anything approaching the needy attachment or the guilt and rejection that are so characteristic of the nuclear family.

While there are clearly exceptions, the extended family generally provides more space and flexibility and far less pressure on each individual, both emotionally and in terms of responsibility. It is particularly beneficial for the elderly and for women and children. Within the extended family, older people are appreciated for their wisdom and experience, and their slower pace does not prevent them from making an important contribution to the community. In our society, by contrast, technological change is so rapid that experience has less and less value. We have transformed the world around us so dramatically that older people have little to offer from their lifetime. Ladakhis who have traveled to the West tell horror stories about the neglect old people suffer, living alone with no one to talk to. "Grandmothers wait for months to see their grandchildren for a few short hours," Gyelong Paldan remarked, "and then get only a small peck on the cheek."

At the same time as the nuclear family excludes old people, it imprisons women. In traditional societies, women do not have to choose between home and work, since the household is the center of the economy and the two realms are one. By contrast, women with families in the modern world have two choices, neither of which is an easy option. They can stay at home with children, not valued for the work they do, or they can do two jobs, typically with no more than token help from their husbands.

All the signs tell us that the nuclear family is not working. The divorce rate, the alienation of adolescents from their parents, the shocking extent of domestic violence and sexual abuse within the family are examples of this breakdown. Psychologists now describe the "dysfunctional family" as the typical family. Even as recently as fifty years ago, the family in the industrial world was healthier and more supportive than it is today. Once, Grandmother lived next door, and there were cousins and aunts nearby; connections to the larger community were stronger and longer-lasting. Now, as the economic arena expands, it is not unusual for a family to live in as many as six different homes while the children are growing up. There's no room for Grandmother any more: physically, economically, or psychologically.

Often when I talk about family with people in the West, they say, "Having my mother living with us is a nice idea, but it just wouldn't work. We'd all go crazy after two or three days." They are right—it wouldn't work very well at the moment. Because of the way our society is structured, having aging parents in the house becomes a burden. But it could work, if we changed our political priorities to give more attention to fundamental human needs.

In stark contrast to the nuclear family, which tends to seal itself off from the outside world, relationships within the Ladakhi family naturally extend themselves into the broader community. It is sometimes hard to say where family ends and community begins. Any woman old enough to be your mother is called "Mother," anyone of the right age to be your brother is called "Brother." We still see remnants of this in industrial society. In the more traditional parts of Sweden and Russia, for example, a child will call any familiar adult "Uncle" or "Auntie."

Most Westerners would agree that we have lost our sense of community. Our lives are fragmented, and in spite of the number of people with whom we come into contact in the course of a day, we are often left feeling sadly alone, not even knowing our neighbors. In Ladakh, people are part of a community that is spiritually, socially, and economically interdependent.

Decentralization is a prerequisite for the rekindling of community in Western society. Mobility erodes community, but as we put down roots and feel attachment to a place, our human relationships deepen, become more secure, and—as they continue over time—more reliable.

The broader sense of self in traditional Ladakhi society contrasts with the individualism of Western culture. A Ladakhi's identity is to a great extent molded by close bonds with other people, and is reinforced by the Buddhist emphasis on interconnectedness. People are supported in a network of relationships that spread in concentric circles around them—family, farm, neighborhood, village. In the West we pride ourselves on our individualism, but sometimes individualism is a euphemism for isolation. We tend to believe that a person should be completely self-sufficient, that he or she should not need anybody else. I have a friend who was divorced the same year her only child left home for school. She was quite naturally unhappy. But she felt that her misery was a sign of weakness, that she should learn to like being on her own, to feel at peace in her empty house.

The closely knit relationships in Ladakh seem liberating rather than oppressive, and have forced me to reconsider the whole concept of freedom. This is not as surprising as it might appear. Psychological research is verifying the importance of intimate, reliable, and lasting relations with others in creating a positive self-image. We are beginning to recognize how this in turn is the foundation for healthy development. Ladakhis score very highly in terms of self-image. It is not something conscious; it is perhaps closer to a total absence of self-doubt, a profound sense of security. This inner security breeds tolerance and an acceptance of others with all their differences.

One summer, when I was doing a study of child development and child care practices in the Zanskar Valley, I asked a group of mothers if they ever worried when a child was late in learning to walk. They roared with laughter: "Why should we worry about a thing like that? They'll learn to walk when they are ready." In mainstream Western culture, we keep increasingly careful percentile charts of our babies' height and weight because we live in a society that is growing ever more insecure and competitive. A generation ago, mothers were told to feed their newborn babies according to a strict schedule, so as not to "spoil" them. A friend of mine tells me that when her baby daughter was crying in her crib from hunger, she would be sitting in the next room, crying too, until she was allowed by the clock to feed her.

The Western monoculture exerts tremendous pressure to conform. At a bus stop in Sweden I was standing next to two little boys

Two sisters. Living in large families and close-knit communities, the Ladakhis are emotionally and psychologically secure.

who were comparing their sport shoes. One of them was in tears while desperately pulling at the inside of his shoe, looking for the label that would show he had the right brand. The damage is obviously on a deeper level when it is our sex, skin color, or age that is not the right brand. In the commercial mass culture the young white male is the cultural ideal. As a result women, minorities, and old people are disadvantaged. We do not have as much individual freedom as we think we have.

While decentralization is the most necessary structural change we must make, it needs to be accompanied by a corresponding change in world view. Increasing ecological distress has clearly demonstrated wide-reaching interconnections in natural systems, but most academic institutions continue to perpetuate ever more narrowly focused specialization. This reductionist perspective is, in fact, one of the root causes of the malaise of industrial culture. Paradoxically, a trend toward smaller-scale political and economic units would help us to develop a broader world view—one based on interconnectedness. Instead of narrowing our vision, an intimate connection to community and place would encourage an understanding of interdependence. When you are dependent on the earth under your feet and the community around you for your survival, you experience interdependence as a fact of daily life. Such a deep experiential understanding of interconnectedness—feeling yourself a part of the continuum of life—contrasts starkly with the analytic, fragmented, and theoretical thinking of modern society.

We need to return to a more empathetic relationship with the living world and learn to see broader patterns, process, and change. Nowadays, one biologist does not speak the same language as another, unless they are both studying the same kind of fruit fly. How can we understand life by breaking it into fragments and freezing it in time? Our static and mechanistic world view has reached its limits, and some scientists—particularly quantum physicists—now speak of a paradigm shift away from the old "building block" view of reality to a more organic one. In direct opposition to the trend in mainstream culture toward greater specialization, we need to actively promote the generalist—the one who sees connections and makes links across different disciplines. In this regard, one of the most hopeful trends is the increasing respect for more feminine values and ways of thinking.

Research into women's thought patterns is substantiating the assertion that the feminine point of view places greater emphasis on relationship and connections, both in terms of empathy and abstract thinking. Such a perspective is obviously not the exclusive property of women, and in recent years men have begun to value more consciously the feminine side of themselves. But for hundreds of years, this more contextual way of thinking and being has been not only neglected, but undermined by industrial culture. The dominant perspective of our society is now out of balance. A shift toward the feminine is long overdue.

This shift would also bring with it an emphasis on experiential knowledge. To a much greater extent than men, women can be said to form their abstractions from personal experience. Interestingly enough, the same can be said of the Ladakhis and many traditional and non-Western cultures. To understand the complexities of the natural world, theory must be grounded in experience. Experiential learning is based in messy reality, with all its paradox and untidiness, its ever-changing pattern, its refusal to conform to our expectations. As such, it inevitably leads to humility. If our studies were conducted less in the laboratory and more in the field—in the fields, in fact—scientific advance would proceed more cautiously. If we learned to examine the potential effects of new technologies in context, over time, we would be less likely to set off destructive chains of unintended effects.

In the West, we tend to live our lives at one remove from reality, relying on images and concepts. As Tashi Rabgyas said after spending a few months in England, "It's amazing how indirect everything is here. They write about the beauty of nature, they talk about it, and everywhere there are potted plants and plastic plants, and pictures of trees on the wall. And all the time television programs about nature. But they don't ever seem to have contact with the real thing."

On my most recent visit to Sweden, I had lunch with my friend Karin in her garden outside Stockholm. A successful lawyer and the mother of two teenage daughters, she had been a volunteer with the Ladakh Project the previous summer and we had become friends.

"Ladakh came home with me," she said. "I keep discovering how deeply it affected me." On her return to Sweden, she had realized the need to make changes in her life. She cut back on her legal practice to do voluntary work for an environmental organization. She slowed her pace, planted a vegetable garden, and started spending more time with her children.

Karin is by no means alone. A movement to build eco-villages is sweeping Sweden: two hundred are already planned, all of them based on renewable energy and the recycling of waste. Increasing numbers of people are choosing to buy organic food and are strengthening the local economy by buying from farmers close to home. The government has committed itself to establishing an environmental accounting system in which the destruction of natural resources will be subtracted from the gross national product.

These changes in Sweden reflect a crucial shift in direction. Throughout the industrial world, people are searching for a better balance with nature. In the process, they are starting to mirror traditional cultures. In fields as diverse as hospice care for the dying and mediation as a way of settling disputes, striking parallels are emerging between the most ancient and the most modern cultures. Just as Ladakhi villagers have always done, increasing numbers of people are making the kitchen the center of their household activity, eating whole foods that are grown naturally, and using age-old natural remedies for their health problems. Even in more subtle ways, such as a reawakened interest in storytelling, a renewed appreciation for physical work, and the use of natural materials for clothing and construction, the direction of change is clear. We are spiraling back to an ancient connection between ourselves and the earth.

The process, however, is often an unconscious one. Our mainstream culture encourages a linear view of progress, one in which the goal is to free ourselves from our past and from the laws of nature. The modern-day mantra "we cannot go back, we cannot go back" is deeply ingrained in our thinking. Of course we could not go back, even if we wanted to, but our search for a future that works is inevitably bringing us back to certain fundamental patterns that are in greater harmony with nature—including human nature.

In our attempts to find ways of living that correspond more closely with our inner selves, some of the greatest advances have been in the area of child rearing. Could this be because it is here that the woman's viewpoint is most strongly felt? Thankfully, the practice of clock-controlled feeding has been abandoned as we have returned to a greater respect for natural instincts; and now both mothers and fathers carry their babies around next to their bodies in postindustrial papooses. We are beginning to learn what the traditional Ladakhis never forgot—that every human being is born deserving unconditional love, and that children can only really flourish in a family system in which there is no need to prove yourself, no need to earn the right to be who you are.

Around the world, in every sphere of life, from psychology to physics, from farming to the family kitchen, there is a growing aware-

ness of the interconnectedness of all life. New movements are springing up, committed to living on a human scale, and to more feminine
and spiritual values. The numbers are growing, and the desire for
change is spreading. These trends are often labeled "new," but, as I
hope Ladakh has shown, in an important sense they are very old.
They are, in fact, a rediscovery of values that have existed for thousands of years—values that recognize our place in the natural order,
our indissoluble connection to one another and to the earth.

READING LIST

Attenborough, R. ed. 1982. *The Words of Gandhi*. New Market Press, N.Y. One of many anthologies of Gandhi's writings.

Badiner, Alan H. 1990. *Dharma Gaia: A Harvest of Essays in Buddhism and Ecology*. Parallax Press, Berkeley. Essays exploring how the holistic view of Buddhism is related to ecological thinking.

Bahro, Rudolf. 1986. *Building the Green Movement*. New Society, Philadelphia. Essays from a leading German Green thinker.

Bellah, Robert N., Richard Madsen, William M. Sullivan, Ann Swidler, Steven Tipton. 1985. *Habits of the Heart: Individualism and Commitment in American Life*. Harper and Row, London, N.Y. This sociological study, based on extensive interviews, looks at how individualism and economic rationality affect community in America.

Berger, Peter. 1974. *Pyramids of Sacrifice*. Basic, New York. Berger questions the sacrifice and destruction that have been brought about by both capitalist and communist development, and examines the roots of both systems in modernism.

Berman, Morris. 1981. *The Reenchantment of the World*. Cornell University Press, Ithaca, New York. An examination of alternatives to the Newtonian world view, both historical and future.

Berry, Thomas. 1988. *The Dream of the Earth*. Sierra Club, San Francisco. Essays on forging a new relation between humanity and the earth.

Berry, Wendell. 1975. *A Continuous Harmony: Essays Cultural and Agricultural*. Harcourt Brace Jovanovich, N.Y.; 1977. *The Unsettling of America*. Sierra Club, San Francisco; 1987. *Home Economics: Fourteen Essays*. North Point Press, San Francisco; 1990. *What Are People For*. North Point Press, San Francisco. Several of the many books by America's most eloquent and prolific defender of traditional rural life and small-scale farming.

Bizimana, N. 1989. *White Man's Paradise: Hell for Africa.* (Available from the author: Grainauer Str. 13, 1000 Berlin 10, Germany.) Autobiographical account of an East African's encounter and subsequent delusion with the culture of Western Europe.

Bodley, John H. 1990 (Third Ed.) *Victims of Progress.* Mayfield, Mountain View, California; 1976. *Anthropology and Contemporary Human Problems.* Cummings Press, Menlo Park, California; 1987. *Tribal Peoples and Development Issues.* Mayfield, Mountain View, California. Thorough examinations of misconceptions about tribal peoples, and the destruction wrought on these cultures by contact with the West.

Boulding, Kenneth E. 1978. *Ecodynamics: A New Theory of Societal Evolution.* Sage Publications, Beverly Hills. A renegade (and ecologically minded) economist's vision of how social and environmental systems interact.

Brown, Lester R. 1981. *Building a Sustainable Society.* W. W. Norton, New York. The founder of the World Watch Institute lays out what he sees as necessary reforms to bring human demands in line with environmental constraints. See also the Worldwatch papers and annual *State of the World.*

Burns, E. Bradford. 1980. *The Poverty of Progress: Latin America in the Nineteenth Century.* University of California Press, Berkeley. Documents the destruction of traditional cultures in Latin America in the face of the onslaught of ideas and gadgets from the North.

Callenbach, Ernest. 1975. *Ecotopia.* Banyan Tree Books, Berkeley; 1981. *Ecotopia Emerging.* Banyan Tree Books, Berkeley. Fictionalized speculation on ecologically sound utopia.

Capra, Fritjof. 1982. *The Turning Point: Science, Society, and the Rising Culture.* Bantam Books, N.Y. This book links the major problems facing the world today to a dangerously narrow world view that has dominated for the last centuries, and outlines a new, more holistic paradigm emerging in a variety of domains.

Covarrubias, Miguel. 1937. *Island of Bali.* Knopf, N.Y. A detailed account of the intricacies of Balinese life, at a time when Western visitors were less abundant than today.

Daly, Herman E., and John B. Cobb, Jr. 1989. *For the Common Good: Redirecting the Economy Toward Community, the Environment, and a Sustainable Future.* Beacon, Boston. An economist and a theologian team up to challenge current economic thinking. They propose protecting people, communities, and the environment by increasing local control, and restricting international trade.

Devall, Bill. 1988. *Simple in Means, Rich in Ends: Practicing Deep Ecology.* Peregrine Books, Salt Lake City. Thoughts on translating non-anthropocentric world views into practice.

Diamond, Irene, and Gloria F. Orenstein, eds. 1990. *Reweaving the World: The Emergence of Ecofeminism.* Sierra Club, San Francisco. A diverse collection of essays affirming the importance of women's experience and knowledge in overcoming patriarchy and healing the earth.

Ehrenfeld, David. 1978. *The Arrogance of Humanism*. Oxford University Press, Oxford, N.Y. Ehrenfeld questions the hubris of humanism. He examines the modern assumptions of ever-increasing material wealth and ever-greater control of nature through technological progress.

Ekins, Paul. 1986. *The Living Economy: A New Economics in the Making*. Routledge and Kegan Paul, New York. This collection of essays from TOES, The Other Economic Summit, critiques the conventional economic paradigm, and presents alternative analyses and visions.

Elgin, Duane. 1981. *Voluntary Simplicity: Toward a Way of Life That Is Outwardly Simple, Inwardly Rich*. William Morrow, New York. An exploration of the personal and planetary effects of living a materially simple lifestyle in industrial society.

Ellul, Jacques. 1964. *The Technological Society*. Random House, New York. (Translated from the French, originally published 1954.) A somewhat difficult to read classic on the continued incursion of technical rationality into all phases of life in industrial civilization.

Fromm, Erich. [1976] 1981. *To Have or To Be*. Bantam, N.Y., London. Two modes of existence struggle fiercely for the spirit of mankind: the having mode, dedicated to aggression and material possession, and the being mode, suffused with love, caring, and a feeling of sufficiency. One of many insightful books by a prolific author.

Fukuoka, Masanobu. 1978. *The One Straw Revolution: An Introduction to Natural Farming*. Rodale, Emmaus, Pennsylvania. Description of a farming system developed over thirty years that minimizes human intervention in the natural order. A classic that has inspired many permaculturists and others.

George, Susan. 1977. *How the Other Half Dies: The Real Reasons for World Hunger*. Allanheld Osmun, Montclair, New Jersey; 1988. *A Fate Worse Than Debt*. Grove Press, N.Y. These books expose the gross inequalities of the current international economic system and the development policies that support it.

Gilligan, Carol. 1982. *In a Different Voice: Psychological Theory and Women's Development*. Harvard University Press, Cambridge, Mass. Gilligan exposes the male bias in psychological testing.

Goldsmith, Edward. 1988. *The Great U-Turn: Deindustrializing Society*. Green Books, Bideford, U.K. A call for radical restructuring of modern society from the editor of *The Ecologist*.

Goodman, Paul, and Percival Goodman. [1947] 1960. *Communitas: Means of Livelihood and Ways of Life*. Random House, New York. Early questioning about the directions of industrial culture; still relevant.

Griffin, David Ray. 1988. *The Reenchantment of Science: Postmodern Proposals*. State University of New York Press, Albany. Essays calling for a replacement of modern dualism and reductionism with a more ecological, organismic, and ultimately spiritual foundation to scientific inquiry.

Griffin, Susan. *Woman and Nature: The Roaring Inside Her*. Harper and Row, New York.

A unique and powerful work that juxtaposes the voice of modern patriarchy with women's voices on a variety of themes of society and nature.

Heilbroner, Robert. 1974. *An Inquiry into the Human Prospect.* W. W. Norton, New York. This book outlines the discrepancies between the material, the cultural, and the social products of advanced industrial society and generally desirable human goals.

Henderson, Hazel. 1971. *Creating Alternative Futures.* G. P. Putnam, New York; and 1981. *The Politics of the Solar Age.* Anchor, Doubleday, New York. An exploration of new directions in economic and political thinking that can help create a more ecologically sound future.

Illich, Ivan. 1971. *Deschooling Society*; 1973. *Tools for Conviviality*; 1974. *Energy and Equity.* Harper and Row, New York. Key works from one of the most insightful and severe critics of industrial society.

Jackson, Wes. 1980. *New Roots for Agriculture.* Friends of the Earth, San Francisco; with Wendell Berry, 1984. *Meeting the Expectations of the Land: Essays in Sustainable Agriculture.* North Point Press, San Francisco; 1987. *Altars of Unhewn Stone: Science and the Earth.* North Point Press, San Francisco. Fundamental questioning of the patterns of thinking that underlie modern industrial agriculture from an agricultural researcher who is investigating the possibilities of radical changes in the way we practice agriculture.

Keller, Evelyn Fox. 1985. *Reflections on Gender and Science.* Yale University Press, New Haven, Connecticut. Essays on how scientific questioning and methods have been shaped by patriarchy and why a feminization of science is needed.

King, Franklin H. [1911] 1973. *Farmers of Forty Centuries; or, Permanent Agriculture in China, Korea, and Japan.* Rodale, Emmaus, Pennsylvania. Description of traditional farming practices that maintained fertility for centuries.

Kohr, Leopold. 1973. *Development Without Aid: The Translucent Society.* Schlocken, N.Y; [1962] 1976. *The Overdeveloped Nations: The Diseconomies of Scale.* Swansea. Early and cogent challenges to the growth and development mystiques.

Lappé, Francis Moore, and Joseph Collins. 1977. *Food First.* Houghton and Mifflin, Boston; with David Kinley. 1980. *Aid as Obstacle: Twenty Questions About Our Foreign Aid and the Hungry.* Institute for Food and Development Policy, San Francisco. A thorough refutation of common beliefs about the causes of hunger; misguided development and political economic policies are most often the important factors.

Leopold, Aldo. [1987] 1949. *A Sand County Almanac, and Sketches Here and There.* Oxford University Press, Oxford, N.Y. Eloquent reflections on the beauty of nature, and philosophical inquiries into the ethics of modern society's relation to nature. Contains well-known essay on Leopold's proposed land ethic.

Lutz, Mark A., and Kenneth Lux. 1988. *Humanistic Economics: The New Challenge.* Bootstrap Press, New York. Challenges the basic assumptions about homo economicus in favor of Gandhian economics.

Macy, Joanna. 1985. *Dharma and Development: Religion as Resource in the Sarvodya Self-help Movement.* Kumarian Press, West Hartford, Connecticut. The role of Buddhism and Buddhist monks and nuns in Sri Lanka's Sarvodya village development movement.

Mander, Jerry. 1978. *Four Arguments for the Elimination of Television*. Morrow, N.Y. Insights into the subtle ways television distorts reality and affects us psychologically. Recommended even for those who are already convinced of the negative aspects of television.

Margolin, Malcolm. 1978. *The Ohlone Way: Indian Life in the San Francisco Monterey Bay Area*. Heyday Books, Berkeley, California. A description of what life was like before the European invasion of California.

Matthiessen, Peter. 1978. *The Snow Leopard*. Viking, New York. Description of an expedition to study snow leopards in Tibetan Buddhist Nepal.

Merchant, Carolyn. 1980. *The Death of Nature: Women, Ecology and the Scientific Revolution*. Harper and Row, New York. The rise in dominance of the mechanistic world view of modern science was accompanied by the increasing exploitation of nature and the domination of women.

Mollison, Bill. 1990. *Permaculture: A Practical Guide for a Sustainable Future*. Island Press, Covelo, California; also, *Permaculture One* and *Permaculture Two*. Design ideas for creating living arrangements that provide a maximum of food, energy, and shelter with a minimum of environmental impact. The Permaculture bible.

Mumford, Lewis. [1934] 1963. *Technics and Civilization*. Harcourt Brace Jovanovich, New York. A history of modern technology and how it has shaped both the external world and human society and culture. Mumford's insights into the powerful force of "technics" are as relevant today as they were in 1934.

Naess, Arne. 1989. *Ecology, Community and Lifestyle: Outline of an Ecosophy*. Cambridge University Press, Cambridge, N.Y. Translated and revised by David Ruthenberg. Deep ecology from the Norwegian philosopher who first coined the term.

Nash, Hugh, ed. 1981. *Progress as if Survival Mattered: A Handbook for a Conserver Society*. Friends of the Earth, San Francisco. Policy suggestions to steer society toward a more ecological footing.

Payer, Cheryl. 1975. *The Debt Trap: The IMF and the Third World*; 1982. *The World Bank: A Critical Analysis*. Monthly Review Press, N.Y. A critical look at two of the major international development institutions and the effects of their policies on the lives of people in the South.

Polanyi, Karl. [1944] 1957. *The Great Transformation: The Political and Economic Origins of Our Time*. Beacon, Boston. A historical perspective on the sweeping changes brought by the reorganization of society around markets.

Pye-Smith, Charles, and Richard North. 1984. *Working the Land: A New Plan for a Healthy Agriculture*. Temple Smith, London. Exposition of the ills of English agriculture and the organic alternative.

Rifkin, Jeremy. 1983. *Algeny*. Viking, N.Y; 1985. *Declaration of a Heretic*. Routledge and Kegan Paul, Boston. A plea for caution and humility in scientific research and technological development.

Roszak, Theodore. 1979. *Person Planet*. Doubleday, Garden City. An excellent exposition of the thesis that the forces that are endangering the environment also threaten individuals and communities. The cures for the personal and the planetary lie in the same direction.

Sahlins, Marshall. 1972. *Stone Age Economics*. Aldine Atherton Inc., Chicago, N.Y. Drawing on a wide range of anthropological study, Sahlins explodes the myth that life for hunter-gatherers was a constant struggle. He also examines exchange relations in preindustrial society and points out many reasons to challenge the "naturalness" of today's conceptions of "economic man."

Sale, Kirkpatrick. 1980. *Human Scale*. Coward, McCann and Geoghegan, New York; 1985. *Dwellers in the Land: The Bioregional Vision*. Sierra Club, San Francisco. An appeal for smaller scale, decentralization, and the reorganization of society to better integrate with the natural world and the real needs of humanity.

Schumacher, E. F. 1973. *Small Is Beautiful: Economics as if People Mattered*. Harper and Row, New York, Blond and Briggs Ltd., London. This seminal work by the father of the Appropriate Technology movement challenges the assumptions of growth, development, and the economic paradigm. Schumacher's vision puts the needs of people before economic efficiency.

Shiva, Vandana. 1988. *Staying Alive: Women, Ecology and Development*. Zed, London. The women and the land of India bear the costs of destructive and short-sighted development.

Snyder, Gary. 1974. *Turtle Island*. New Directions, N.Y; 1977. *The Old Ways: Six Essays*. City Lights Books, San Francisco; 1990. *The Practice of the Wild*. North Point Press, San Francisco. Also many volumes of poetry. An internationally renowned poet who has written poetry and essays for the last four decades on, among other things, nature, spirituality, and the wisdom of tradition.

Spretnak, Charlene. 1986. *The Spiritual Dimension of Green Politics*. Bear and Co., Santa Fe. The importance of spiritual wisdom in regaining a more healthy relationship to the earth.

Turnbull, Colin M. 1961. *The Forest People*. Chatto & Windus, London. Life and culture of the traditional inhabitants of the rainforests of central Africa.

Van der Post, Laurens. 1961. *The Heart of the Hunter*. Hogarth Press, London (African Bushman folklore); 1974. *A Far-off Place*. Morrow, New York; 1953. *The Face Beside the Fire: A novel*. Morrow, New York. Fiction set in traditional Africa.

The Ladakh Project/International Society for Ecology and Culture is a non-profit organization. For more information, please write to:

The Ladakh Project/ISEC, P.O. Box 9475, Berkeley, CA 94709

The Ladakh Project/ISEC, 21 Victoria Square, Clifton, Bristol BS8 4ES, United Kingdom

The Ladakh Project/ISEC, Leh, Ladakh, Jammu & Kashmir, India

INDEX

199